EARLY ENDORSEMENTS FOR
Plant Whatever Brings You Joy

"… as luscious as a peony in full bloom. Thank you for walking me in the garden of your heart."

— Dawna Markova, Ph.D., author of *I Will Not Die an Unlived Life* and co-author of *Random Acts of Kindness*

"Gardens have been with us since the time of Eden. They teach, they nourish the body and the soul, they beautify. *Plant Whatever Brings You Joy* is also a garden — of delight, of wisdom and of sustenance."

— Martin Rutte, co-author *Chicken Soup for the Soul at Work*

"This is such a deeply personal book. It is so much a part of you, and the passion and energy are tangible. It is part of the beauty of this book that I suspect your readers will want to share their own stories. It is a testament to the skillful writing style, seemingly so easy and natural, and the life affirming lessons to be considered that your readers will make this book their own; it is just that kind of book: a book to treasure."

— Philip Bewley, Philip's Garden Blog

"This delightful book of easy-reading stories will plant much wisdom in the garden of your life. Simple and profound, it will help awaken your own graceful flowering!"

— Brooke Medicine Eagle, author of *Buffalo Woman Comes Singing* and *The Last Ghost Dance*

"I heard your voice and your laugh, saw your sparkling eyes … and I could feel and see every single experience you described. I was there in your life stories with you. As they say … I laughed and I cried. I LOVE YOUR BOOK!"

— Joanna Chernauskas, author of *Because You Care*

"Through metaphor and story, Kathryn Hall calls forth images of what it means to cultivate our inner garden. This revealing collection sheds light on the soul's yearning for beauty, joy, and meaning wherever you are.

— Alan Briskin, author of *The Stirring of Soul in the Workplace*

"This gentle book has made me more aware of the wisdom available in all small acts — a delight that stays with you — and a large gift."

— Margaret J. Wheatley, author of *Turning to One Another*

"Women are nourished by other women's stories. Hall links metaphors she has drawn from gardening with stories from her colorful life experiences — inspirational words of wisdom to guide others through their life transitions. Her humor, authenticity, and courage shine through each story, and her probing questions at each chapter's end invite the writer to move more deeply into the process of self-transformation."

— Patty Montgomery, author of *Mythmaking*

WHAT READERS ARE SAYING ABOUT
plantwhateverbringsyoujoy.com

"Oh dear Kathryn … you are a wise woman, connected with the universe. An 'old soul' perhaps? With heart of gold and malleable arms, you embrace the world around you."

— Joey Randall, Michigan

"Further evidence of reasons you're one of my heroines, Kathryn. Beautifully told and beautifully reasoned. You consistently bring good things to light, and I'm grateful for your unique insights and stories."

— David Perry, Seattle

"*Plant Whatever Brings You Joy blog by Kathryn Hall*. How can you not love a blog with this name? Kathryn's polished, yet accessible writing style inspires me to sign up for writing classes! Her posts are varied in subject matter from garden art, garden tools, vegetable gardening, recipes and much more. A common theme that I gravitate to is how Kathryn finds joy in most everything in life and in the garden."

— Shirley Bovshow, host, *Garden Police*, Discovery Home Channel

"Firstly, I have to say I truly enjoy your inimitable wit. You always astound me with your use of words. You say everything 'in a lady-like way' … I love your sense of humor. You always tell a simple story with such panache!"

— Brenda Kula, Texas

"You are so funny. I have been reading for some time now and hooked … It's easy to read your style. It flows nicely. Thank you for a nice evening of entertaining stories in your backyard."

— Anna, Washington

"Hi Kathryn! I always look forward to opening up this site and drooling all over your photos of intense physical—and spiritual—beauty!"
— Suzette Marlowe, Hawaii

"Your blog is fantastic. I can tell your heart is truly in what you do and it's very inspiring."
— Tonia, North Carolina

"I was so touched by your story. Thank you for sharing such a poignant story. You are truly a remarkable person."
— Carolyn, Chicago

"Wow, Kathryn, This is powerful stuff. I experienced the shivers just reading your eloquent words … Thank you."
— Debra Prinzing, author *Stylish Sheds and Elegant Hideaways*, Los Angeles

"Your sense of humour is great—I got hooked [on] this blog for good."
— Ewa Marie, Poland

"Congratulations on the world-wide readership you are gaining! I'm very happy it brings you such joy, because you bring joy to your readers as well."
— Lori Holstein, Salt Lake City, UT

"I just gave a friend whose husband is dying of cancer the address for your blog. Such beauty will be peaceful for her."
— Loma Wilkins, Norwich, New York

EX LIBRIS

_____

_____

Plant Whatever Brings You Joy

BLESSED WISDOM FROM THE GARDEN

Kathryn Hall

PLANT WHATEVER BRINGS YOU JOY
Blessed Wisdom from the Garden
Copyright © Kathryn Hall 2010

PUBLISHER'S CATALOGING-IN-PUBLICATION DATA
Hall, Kathryn J., 1943-
   Plant whatever brings you joy : blessed wisdom from the garden /
Kathryn Hall. -- 1st ed. -- Ukiah, CA : Estrella Catarina, c2010.
   p. ; cm.
   ISBN: 978-0-9815570-0-7
   1. Gardening. 2. Spiritual life. 3. Meditations. 4. Gardening--
Religious aspects. 5. Nature--Religious aspects. I. Title.
   SB455.3 .H35 2010
   635.01--dc22 1008ISBN-13: 978-0-9815570-0-7
   ISBN-10: 0-9815570-0-7

FIRST EDITION
PRINTED IN THE UNITED STATES OF AMERICA.
1 3 5 7 9 8 6 4 2

BLESSED WISDOM FROM THE GARDEN

1.
Remember that all seeds have their own rate of return.

2.
Fiercely guard the seedlings.

3.
Know which plants you grow well.

4.
Leave wild, undisturbed corners in your garden.

5.
Bask in the light.

6.
Repot the rootbound for growth and expansion.

7.

Cherish the beauty of the season.

8.

Gently guide the tender vine, else it become
wild, tangled and impossible.

9.

Cherish the precious volunteers.

10.

Encourage potential.

11.

Bring gentleness and gratitude to your harvesting.

12.

Plant whatever brings you joy!

13.

Rotate your crops.

14.

Honor the seed planted by another hand.

15.

Never underestimate the power of one tiny seed.

16.
Nurture, nurture, nurture.

17.
Wear the right garb.

18.
Aim for beauty.

19.
Take comfort in the mystery.

20.
Never pull up and discard what you cannot identify.

21.
Recognize when a plant's life is spent and
be willing to let it go.

22.
Use the right tool for the job.

23.
Resist the temptation to plant more than you can care for.

24.
Stand firmly rooted in the ground.

25.
Share generously your bounty.

26.
Build sound fences.

27.
Feel not obliged to make good use of
every ripe fruit on the vine.

28.
Mistake not one plant for another.

29.
Appreciate small returns.

30.
Let your ground lie fallow.

31.
Deeply till the hardened ground.

32.
Prune rigorously with faith new life will return.

33.

When pulling up weeds get the root.

34.

Take heart in the plant that survives all odds.

35.

Judge not the flower by its bud.

36.

Distinguish friends from predators.

37.

Plan your activities in harmony with the seasons.

38.

Invite a friend to keep you company.

39.

Test and amend your soil.

40.

Allow ample space for the breadth of your vision.

41.

Trim unwieldy branches.

42.

Plant sun-loving plants in the sun;
plant shade-loving plants in the shade.

43.

Reframe all error as learning.

44.

Clean up after a storm.

45.

Move gently among bees.

46.

Invest in trees.

47.

Harvest seeds for future gardens.

48.

Recycle everything.

49.

Celebrate the fruits of your labors.

50.

Cultivate plants which attract lovely company.

51.

Feed and water at optimum times.

52.

Know and include a wide variety of
species in your garden.

For Antonia, the most precious flower in my garden

FOREWORD

While reading Kathryn Hall's enchanting stories a line from poet William Stafford's "When I Met My Muse" came to mind:

> " 'I am your own way of looking at things,' she said
> 'When you allow me to live with you every
> glance around you will be a kind of salvation.'
> And I took her hand."

Kathryn Hall's stories are a generous invitation to discover our own way of looking at things. By letting her take our hand we are gently guided towards seeing the small in the large. By shifting our attention downward our own way to salvation is illuminated through her. "What kindles our joy and our compassion?" she asks. "What makes the moment immeasurably rich?" "How are our hearts nurtured by the company we each keep each day?"

The company she invites us to spend time with involves a host of unlikely and delightful guests. These 'strangers in our midst' are shown to have enlivened her world in wondrous ways.

Her evocative images are a reminder that for far too long we have allowed our world to be illuminated by the sharp glare of the headlight. The paradox being that this search for clear vision has also blinded many of us to the many subtle and mysterious ways of the world that Kathryn describes.

By lighting a candle she reintroduces us to a time-honored but forgotten way to wisdom that can come only through 'slow learning'. In a world of fast knowledge, fast food and fast company these stories need to be read slowly and often. They serve as an antidote reminding us that recognizing and living our gifts is not the final step but the first one.

The difficult work is yet to come. And it involves creating our own garden by building the soil and cultivating an appreciative attention so that the seed of potential that is our gift has the opportunity to flourish and grow.

And it is in this less glamorous, but nonetheless profoundly important work, that Kathryn serves as such a wise host and guide. The titles of her many ways of tending the garden tell the story we need to learn.

Too often we set standards that are too high for ourselves and miss the very thing that we are looking for. "Plant whatever gives you joy," Kathryn says. The difficulty she draws us to is not to work harder but with a greater sense of pleasure and ease. "Resist the temptation to plant more than you can care for." Instead of going wide, go down by "deeply tilling the hardened ground." The virtues she calls forth are ones of patience, gratitude, aliveness and an observant eye.

In this respect her words are like small buds that flower in the presence of those things that bring her closer to those wild undisturbed corners of her own observant life. When we yield to our own heart's deep longing then the longing that is the world can meet us there and in this space between, grace enters in.

> When William Stafford met his muse
> "Her voice belled forth, and the
>   sunlight bent. I felt the ceiling arch, and
>   knew that the nails up there took a new grip
>   On whatever they touched."

While Kathryn is open and responsive in the way she receives her world, her voice is also bold and forthright as she tells us what she has felt and seen.

We learn that the unconditional love we give to that little patch of ground that is our garden is something to grow out from. It helps us learn to live and love a larger more imperfect world with courage and acceptance later on.

Michael Jones
composer, pianist, speaker,
author of *Creating an Imaginative Life*

ACKNOWLEDGEMENTS

I am deeply grateful to Spirit for inspiring me with this vision and to my Self for following through. And I extend my deepest gratitude to the many people who have walked this publishing path with me in the various stages of the unfolding of this book. I am grateful for the loving people who read the final manuscript and to those who offered their caring support, including Pamela Polland, Cornelia Gerken, Kathlene Carney, Justine Daniel, Veronica Fall, Joanna Chernauskas, Kathryn Phillips, Dick Richards, Anita Bruzzese, Betsy Pinter, Patty Montgomery, Marsha Mello, Judy Niderost, my beloved father, Nelson Hall, Antonia Hall, and especially to Philip Bewley, whose enthusiasm gave me the final push. I will be forever grateful for the beautifully rich design and graphics of the very talented Bill Greaves.

I owe a special thanks to my friend Paul Scicchitano who sat on a beach in Florida and offered his edits and believed in this book. I appreciate the conversations I have had with those whose invaluable input guided me along the way, among them fab webguy, Karl Knelson; publishers Steven Piersanti, Siegmar Gerken and Marc Allen; executive editor Jeevan Sivasubramaniam; and agents Michael Larson and June Clark who constructively and generously weighed in, and Laurie Fox for her warm encouragement from the outset. Thanks also to Diana Cruppi, and to McNaughton & Gunn for their patient guidance, and to the kind folks at Cypress House. Most of all I am so very grateful for the thousands of readers who faithfully visit my blog **plantwhateverbringsyoujoy.com.** It was with your comments, love and support that I have brought this book into actual being. Lastly, it would be a travesty not to thank my current fabulous clients Marshall Goldsmith with whom I've been blessed to work with and learn from over much of the last five years and Harvey Mackay who told me a long time ago, "It's risky not to take a risk." Thank you all from the essence of my heart.

Plant Whatever
Brings You Joy

INTRODUCTION

For over three decades it has been my daily habit to spend a part of each early morning in the garden. I have loved this simple practice as it has enabled me to begin the day breathing in the fresh morning air, awakening and renewing my body and preparing me for the day's work. It has also served as a lovely transition from the night's dreamstate to the workaday world, a perfect time to be thoughtful about what blessed wisdom the garden has to offer. I've always found that the simplest act such as pulling weeds or pruning roses stirs in me the most profound insights about the nature of life, and I trust that all the gardeners in the world who chance upon this book will know exactly what I mean.

As a successful gardening blogger I've had the opportunity to meet men and women around the world who share my passion for the simple, quiet joys the garden has to offer. Each of us has discovered the garden to be a place of rich renewal and of deep optimism. From this natural treasure store I've attempted to extract the most barebones wisdoms with the hope and intention of offering a simple tool which might resonate and take root in the hearts and souls of readers and upon which they might draw at any opportune moment. If I have done my joyous task well the reader will find his or her own interpretations to be highly and perfectly unique. May pondering these lessons from the garden bring you ever closer to your own truths and to your own precious heart.

Love and gardening blessings,

Kathryn xoxo

REMEMBER THAT ALL SEEDS HAVE
THEIR OWN RATE OF RETURN

The earliest seeds of *Plant Whatever Brings You Joy* emerged shortly after my daughter left home for college and I moved north to Mendocino where I almost immediately started working on a garden. It was the first time in a long time I had lived alone, and I found I landed in the woods with an insatiable passion for experimenting with all kinds of new plants. It was there I discovered the delicate columbine, the beauty of blue canterbury bells, the joys of growing pink, lavender and white cosmos, and the thrill of scented honeysuckle. Early mornings found me already out among my plants, like as not still in a bathrobe and slippers, anxiously seeing what new thing had emerged or changed from the day before. There was always something. In this morning ritual I began seeing the obvious connection between what I was learning in the garden and how that same lesson held true in other areas of my life, and I began to take mental notes. Later I was inspired enough to purchase a bound journal where I began writing down what I was noticing.

Thus the inception of this book.

I had the luxury of taking years, actually, of making these observations and at some point I began to very tentatively share some of these ideas with close friends. Consistently faces lit up and people nodded and smiled and I began to blow hope and faith into sharing my vision.

Evolution of the project turned up in unexpected places. I took a workshop with a woman who described the phenomenon of "parallel jobs". She described musicians whose souls were longing for expression who had jobs as DJ's or set designers who longed to act. This struck a cord, and I began to wonder if perhaps I was carrying some of this parallel longing in my life as a publicist. This was a job I believed in and loved, but it was also true that all the while "my book" was in the shadows.

I began to publish articles. Tiny tendrils were emerging from the earth.

Then a wonderful opportunity came at a seemingly strange time. Just at the time in my personal life my grandmother was catapulting towards heaven, I was in my business life conversing in cyberspace with a colleague in London who was taking a kind of survey about business travel. I emailed back that while I didn't necessarily do a lot of business travel, I had actually begun a second book, on that very subject. You can imagine my surprise and delight when this editor wrote back to me and asked how much material I had! Next thing I knew I had been hired to write about all the ways in which one might stay healthy while on the road, a subject I loved writing about and could readily contribute to. This was my official launch into being published in a book, a lofty start, indeed, as the publisher was a well-known British firm.

My inner flower grew.

Life had taken me to many new gardens over this period of time and while I cherished "my gardening book" still it seemed to be in somewhat of a dormant period.

An old close friend would remind me now and then, saying she hoped I would continue with this dream, and once she sent me a birthday card she herself had designed. On the cover she had drawn a lovely gold tree with deep and abundant roots with a large chestnut lying below the tree and a myriad of twinkling stars in the sky. Underneath she had written an Ani DiFranco quote, "I will not be afraid to let my talent shine!" Inside she wrote, "Happy Birthday, Kathryn! In the year of the risk".

I don't know what risks I took that year, but it wasn't this book. Still slumbering under that gold tree inside the chestnut, undoubtedly.

Then there was stirring in the roots of my book tree.

One Christmas my darling daughter happened to send me a gardening journal for Christmas. On the cover was a bunny holding a rake and hoe. I knew she was thinking of my book and my love for that project when she chose it and I was touched at her loving thoughtfulness. I thanked her and told her I was going to dedicate the journal to seeing me through on my book.

There are only two entries in the journal. The first states the purpose of the journal and an affirmation for what I saw for my book, written in the present tense, as if it were already happening.

The second entry was written after I returned from a conference in New Mexico where I heard the presentation of an author who revealed to the audience that her book had actually sat in her desk drawer for ten years. I felt the goosebumps on my skin as I listened.

I returned home charged up, determined and committed. The old Goethe quote had long been taped to the top of my telephone when I first began my book publicity business:

"Whatever you can do
Or think you can
Begin it
Boldness has genius, power and magic in it."

I began to act from that place. Clearly the tree had sprouted from its long incubation.

The plant had taken root. I began my blog and over time found a worldwide readership, for which I am incredibly grateful. And now. A book.

Within each big dream are many many seeds and stages of growth. Some seeds fall on barren ground. Some are caught in a sudden breeze of inspiration and grace, falling back to solid ground and everything that is needed to bring it to lovely fruition.

What seeds lie within you that long for all the right ingredients to bloom to glory?

FIERCELY GUARD THE SEEDLINGS

My mother and father met and married when they were very young. When I was soon in her womb my father was called to war. The names of the battles in which he partook reverberate throughout our history today. Normandy Beach. Battle of the Bulge. His war story thankfully ends in his participation in the victory parade down the Champs Elysees with the liberation of the French people. Though my father survived the war, a young marriage enduring the long separation and stresses of the war did not. Another seedling gone awry. I would be in my twenties when I was at last reunited in his arms and heart and we could look in each other's eyes and weep for the loss of each other for all those years. I grew up without the benefit of his fierce protection and suffered as one might expect. However it was my great personal good fortune to have been blessed with loving and devoted grandparents who had my best interests at heart.

The truth is all children are at risk. But some are much more vulnerable, especially those not having a loving family member to watch out for them as I. We know who they are. They have no adult in their lives who really has their back. It grieves me deeply to think of them. They are lying in their beds as I write, listening to an angry fight in the next room. They bury their heads deeper into their pillows trying not to hear. Their hope is in becoming still and invisible, hoping the anger, the rage, the danger will not spill into their rooms. Some of them are reading this page and tears well in their eyes that someone understands their fear and pain. Who will reach out to them? To whom do they actually turn?

I started working with children when I was a child myself. Maybe it was because I was the eldest, and was used to having younger siblings? Maybe because I knew firsthand our needs. But by the time I was nine I was happily gathering and organizing the children in my southern California neighborhood into staging performances. I assigned them bits of poetry to memorize, or songs to sing. I chose my next door neighbor's front porch as our stage. They had the perfect flat lawn facing the porch where we could set up every chair we could scrounge for the audience. (I would recite the poem about Orphan Annie. "Little Orphan Annie's come to our house to stay, to wash the cups and saucers and sweep the crumbs away ..." which ended, "And the goblins will get ya' if you don't watch out.")

This thread of working with children has played a large role in my life. I taught Sunday School as a teen, lovingly teaching the parables of Jesus, and the songs I came to love as a child, my favorites being "This Little Gospel Light of Mine" and most especially "Jesus Loves the Little Children," an inclusive theme prevalent in my life to this day. "Red and yellow, black and white, they are precious in His sight."

The year before I went off to college I worked in a day care center where I had deep latitude to be creative in organizing creative activities for children. After college I worked with children in a recreation department, running an Arts and Crafts and Dramatics Program. I returned to teaching when my daughter was a small child, running an after-school Spanish program sponsored by the PTA with a friend in four schools in Northern California. Later I formally developed and ran a Spanish program for a private school for two years. For a year I worked as a teacher's aide as a liaison between three distinct cultures: the black children from a neighboring community, the houseboat children from the docks of Sausalito, and the children who lived "up on the hill". I organized a gospel choir and a drill team for these children in our spare time. Always, always I have created the opportunity to work with precious children. And the love and gratitude and wonder and laughter and joy that was bestowed on me as a result cannot be tallied.

None of these programs were high paying jobs. Some of them were done as a volunteer. What if none of these programs existed?

These are the precious, vulnerable seedlings in our midst needing our attention, our protection, our guidance, our involvement, our caring. Are you a child who could organize the neighborhood kids into creative afterschool activities? Could you approach the PTA and ask them to sponsor an afterschool program at your school? Are there neighborhood recreation centers in your area, and if not, why not? And what could you do about that? Are you an aide in a school whose job is strictly defined, or so you think, but you know you could be doing more, that would not only benefit children, but breathe new life into your job as well? Is there a child at risk needing you? Is it a child next door? or your own?

Do you know of a child needing fierce protection but you say nothing, contributing to a culture of silence, rather than taking a stand on behalf of the child? Do you fear rocking the boat? Do you fear repercussion? Is there a fearful child living still within you that needs to be heard and healed so that you can own your power and protect other children? If so, where can you seek and find the healing you need? And how, once healed, could you reach out to the children in your life whose pain you know because you have been there and done that? It is through this compassionate embrace that we ultimately find our healing and resurrection and we become the gardeners, the healers, the protectors of the vulnerable seedlings with whom we share our lives.

KNOW WHICH PLANTS
YOU GROW WELL

(My love affair with chickens began when I was a small girl living in the undeveloped mountain terrain of Southern California. We lived on a farm, and we had horses, goats and a pen full of chickens, as well as a cat here and there and a cocker spaniel named Cherry. I don't think we actually owned the dog, but she was often about. One very early photo of me shows me sporting a large ruffled sunbonnet, carrying a small woven basket, full to the brim with chicken eggs, which I had gathered myself.

I was the keeper of the chickens, the one who cared deeply about them. When they managed to scamper through holes in the fence I was the one who would track them down in the orchard, who caught them gently, and lovingly put them back where they belonged in the safety of their pen and flock.)

Simply put, I adore chickens, and, I know the value of a good rooster.

One such rooster was my beloved Chanticleer, whom I first spotted at the bottom of our road in the woods of Northern California. He was a marvelous little Bantam of abundant colors. Reddish browns and dark shimmering greens and iridescent blacks abounded in his full and splendid tail. But he was not alone. Not at all. He had the companionship of a rather scroungy white hen for whom he appeared to be caring. They had set up camp along a stream that emptied into a culvert below the adjacent road, apparently finding plenty to eat in the forest, and sleeping comfortably in trees for safety (or so they thought) at night. No one could account for where they might have come from, and no one really seemed to care. Chickens. What's the fuss?

All my alarms were going off. Chickens alone in the woods! That can't be! I bought chicken feed at the local feed store and caught their keen attention by daily tossing them a handful or two, all the while wondering what more I should do. Were they lost? Did they belong to someone? No one seemed to know, or care. I brought down a large wire cage from my property and set it near their little camp, placing corn just in front of the door. Each day I replenished the corn, trying to get them used to the idea that a cage might be a nice place to be.

One such morning I was saddened to see white feathers strewn along the road's edge and the urgency of my mission heightened dramatically.

This day I placed corn inside the cage. Then I tied a white cotton string to the door of the cage and walked several yards away. The little rooster was beside himself. He circled the cage again and again trying to figure out how to get the corn without entering the cage. Finally his hunger won out and he entered the cage and I softly drew the door shut by pulling on my end of the string. Not a happy fellow inside. Now how to get him home? I stood waiting, trusting, and within two minutes a woman I knew pulled up our road. I gave thanks, and flagged her down and she helped me place the cumbersome cage back into my truck and up the hill went my captive rooster to his new (and safe) abode.

A rooster. I own a rooster. I bought books, crash coursing on chickens. I learned chicken wire keeps chickens *in*, not predators *out*. You really have to lock down chickens at night. What to do?

By day Chanticleer was free to happily roam about the gardens. And when at dusk the wild turkeys alighted in the highest branches of the large pine trees that surrounded our property, taking refuge, I knew it was time for Chanti to go back into his (temporary) cage for the night. Not really knowing him well in regard to whether he would bite, I would shoo him around the garden with my long skirt, holding out the edges trying to direct him where I wanted him. (Where are the Border Collies when you need them?) Usually I won, but on occasion he would escape into a tree and I would have to rest content that probably no predator could get him there, and none did. I invited a young man from 4-H

Club to my house and he taught me how to pick him up. Apparently people who work with chickens routinely pick them up by their feet and hold them upside down. And it works. Chickens become very still. (Wouldn't you?) I personally found it demeaning, but it allowed me to see that Chanti was a good soul, and had no mean intentions. This gave me the courage to actually pick him up each evening, by simply placing my hands over his wings and holding them down to his sides. And thus began the strange chapter of putting him safely inside a small portable dog kennel at night (safe from all wild creatures), which I popped in the back of my closed truck until I rose early and set him free. Safe at last.

Having conquered my fear of my own rooster, I next went shopping for his new companion, our precious Henny Penny, a small brown Bantie hen sporting black and white polka dots, as cute as cute can be. Unfortunately, when I discussed my intentions for her with the feed store guys (always an infinite source of practical information) they warned me not to let the two of them out together! Why not? I asked. "You can't have just one rooster and one hen! He'll Wild Thing her to death!" Oh, my.

Eventually I took the chance and apparently Chanti was an old thing (you should have seen his feet) and slightly senile, as he would forget what he was doing half way through his occasional wild dance on Henny Penny's back and his attention would divert on some tasty worm or bug making its way through the grass. And they would both continue on with whatever they had been doing just prior. They were charming beyond measure as they pecked and scratched their way through the nasturtiums and jasmine and oleander of the front gardens. They never strayed far, they always instinctively stayed under bushes or trees so as not to catch the attention of an overhead hawk or other predator. They dug large cool holes in the soft dirt and sunk their bodies into the damp earth, becoming very still. Occasionally I lost sight of them and I would run outside and call. "Henny Penny, where are you?" And I would hear the gentlest of clucking under a bush here or there, utterly enchanting.

There is great wisdom in the simple knowing what it is you love, that you do well.

LEAVE WILD, UNDISTURBED CORNERS IN YOUR GARDEN

When I was 17 and living with my family on the western banks of Puerto Rico, in a passionate moment, I wrote the following poem:

Oh, for a lonely island lost
For quiet solitude on some bright shore
To watch, unseen, the ocean offer up
Surrenderings of the sea, forevermore.

Years later an artist I knew offered to frame my poem, illustrating it with little shells and bits of sand. I still take pleasure in knowing this came from me at such a tender age. One could say it is rife with teenage angst, the longing of a young girl for her own space, her own ideas, her own life away from parental eyes and ears and minds and expectations. No doubt it was in part the result of being steeped in a tropical paradise, lying under huge full moons, browned by the Caribbean sun, lulled by the unstoppable crashing of large blue waves on the nearby shore, enchanted by riding horseback on the beaches, cast into a foreign culture so radically different from my New England high school!

More likely, however, another thread in my internal process is reflected in Rumi's oft-quoted:

Out beyond ideas of wrongdoing and rightdoing,
there is a field. I'll meet you there.

For all the delving we do, for all the Inner Child work, the Shadow work, the poking around, the self discovery, there will always be, as Einstein told us, the inevitability of mystery. Sheer mystery. Try as we will, we cannot know everything. There will be more on the other side, when the veil of illusion is lifted, when we are at last home in the comfort of all that is. If Emerson was correct, that our birth is but a sleep and a forgetting, what must death be?

I am told that in Scotland and Ireland the old farmers always leave wild and undisturbed corners in their gardens, where they sow nothing, out of respect for The Little People, to give them a place to be. What wild undisturbed corners do you leave within you or within your partner, your children, your parents, your closest friends? What is left respectfully and quietly for passive cultivation, for privacy, for the imagination, for discovery, for serendipity, for faith, for secrecy, for grace, for reverence, for the untapped, for the future, for the unknowable and the unknown?

BASK IN THE LIGHT

Upon being graduated from college in the mid-sixties in Ohio I found myself on the brink of an overwhelming reality. I was about to go out into the world on my own, earn a living and become a working part of society. With my degree in English tucked under my arm, I set out to answer ads for work I thought might be appropriate. I had already rejected an opportunity to go into the Peace Corps having discovered they intended for me to work in a medical clinic in South America. Having intentionally taken a class in Teaching English as a Foreign Language, this made no sense to me whatsoever. I rejected their idea as a bureaucratic lack of imagination and logic. So I explored instead the two opportunities that seemed to present themselves: to teach in an institution for disturbed children or in a black all-girls' public school in the Hough area of Cleveland. I chose the latter.

Having only one semester of student teaching under my belt, entering a large black urban school system was quite intimidating, especially as I was only 21 years old. There were no meetings. I was taken into a large closet full of shelves of books by an administrator and handed a stack of different books. The only instructions I was given were, "All of your students are graded according to their abilities. Pick the right book for the right class." That was it. The books were largely dilapidated, there were not nearly enough, and there seemed to be no rhyme or reason to the various "levels" of the books—nor to the supposed levels to which the girls had been ascribed.

As fate would have it, the building in which our school was housed had previously served as an all-girls' school for a local Catholic church, and subsequently the bathrooms in the school were fitted only for girls. In the wisdom of the local school officials, a public school was created for these all black girls, who were siphoned off from a co-ed school, and they and their parents were largely disgruntled with the arrangement. The classroom I was assigned was a very small room, so small, in fact, that the desks were piled up so close together that there was barely room to move down the aisles. As I anticipated, this close seating only invited discipline problems, only adding to the frustration of the situation.

In spite of the physical limitations, I shortly came to love the girls despite all the bureaucratic roadblocks put in my way. And my connection with them accelerated rapidly when, frustrated with a system that did not provide the basic teaching tools these girls really needed, I decided to just throw out the books. One day I found myself spontaneously teaching the girls grammar through rhythm. No one had ever shown me this technique before. But I found myself writing a sentence on a board and I began clapping. The girls clapped with me. I would shout out, "Subject!" and the girls somehow intuitively began accessing information from a different part of their brains, and they would tell me the subject. "Verb!" And the verb would magically express from their mouths, all the while clapping along. Something amazing was happening. We had tapped into something fundamental, something we shared, something we loved. Rhythm.

After this day classes were different. Not only were the girls enjoying English class, we were really connecting. Some of the girls came up to me in tears, telling me they had never had a teacher like me before. Some even invited me to their homes. I was very touched and felt a deep inner joy that I had somehow found a way to reach my students.

Sadly, next to that joy was my growing awareness that I had stepped inside a job that I was not qualified for primarily because I was very inexperienced, coupled with the critical fact that I did not have the professional structure externally to support me. I felt the girls deserved more and better. I felt I was on my own. I struggled between the two realities. Connecting with the girls. Feeling abandoned by the system. Feeling there was nowhere to turn, and frankly, like no one really cared.

On a Monday morning following a particularly excruciating soul searching weekend, I entered my small classroom. On the opposite wall from the door was a bank of large classroom windows, however the windows on the bottom half were pebble glass, installed to prevent students from being distracted by anything going on outside. On the smooth dark wooden ledge in the middle of that span of windows was a plant I had placed only days before to bring a small bit of life to the classroom. I drew in a startled breath as my eyes lighted on this plant. Over the weekend this plant had grown a very long and unnaturally extended stem so that it could reach upward and catch the light from the clear paned windows above. I could not take my eyes off this plant and instantly my eyes filled with tears and I knew my answer. I had to leave. As much as I was coming to care about these girls, I was not the one to meet their deep needs. This was not the place, nor the time for me to share my gifts. My resignation was as simple as going into an office and informing them that I found the situation untenable and that I would not be returning.

How many of us are choosing to remain in situations that are not right for us, that deprive us of the air and light and love and support we need to bring ourselves to full growth and fruition, and to be of the greatest service? Dear ones, fear not asking for what you deserve in order to bring your best selves to your own life and to this hungry, compassionate and needing planet that sustains us and that we must now sustain. Dare to bask in the light, whatever that is for you.

REPOT THE ROOTBOUND FOR
GROWTH AND EXPANSION

Leaving my first job in Cleveland I shortly made my way to Columbus where I took a job helping to run an afterschool program at a city recreation center. While it was gratifying working with kids, once again I found working within the overlying system to be restrictive and oppressive. The truth is I was suffocating in a conservative climate. I tussled with administrators after defending one of the boys who was dismissed from school because his "hair was too long". It was a quarter inch down his neck beyond a traditional short cut. I was young and ready for the world and impatient with those who held restrictive power.

I recall Andy Warhol coming to Columbus and I was thrilled. I was in the minority. Bob Dylan performed at Ohio State. Then came the Mamas and the Papas. I was so ready for it all. But my Ohio peers and counterparts looked on in bewilderment. I *so* did not belong in Columbus, Ohio. My growth would have been stunted had I continued to stay. I knew it. San Francisco beckoned like a silent beacon of momentous proportions. Thousands of young people from all over the country were honing in on the San Francisco Bay Area. It was a mass exodus out of the heartland. Clearly we were responding to some deep inner call that now was the time and we were the ones. We hardly had a choice. We just went.

In January 1967 I surrendered to the call and set out from Ohio for San Francisco with one of my best friends, a black man, named Luther. I had met Luther some years before at a small coffeehouse called The Blind Owl in my college town, where the likes of Buffy St. Marie, Gordon Lightfoot and the famous (and dear) blind folksinger Jose Feliciano had all passed through and performed. As guitar players and singers Luther and I shared this unlikely early history. Somehow the fact that civil rights workers were flooding the South, that our country was in political and historical turmoil and that I might be in some potential danger as a young blonde white girl crossing the country with a black man never once entered my mind. To me, he was Luther, my friend. It has only been in the last year or so that Luther (as we are still friends) confessed that he was doing the worrying for both of us! Apparently he was keenly aware of the way we were looked at in various stops we made in conservative towns as we made our way towards our promised land. I was totally oblivious to it all. I rested in the security and trust and strength of our friendship.

I will never forget the night we arrived in San Francisco and we drove across the Bay Bridge, the lighted arching spans of the bridge stretching into a black sky spotted with twinkling stars, the dark bay beneath us. This glorious and liberating image and experience has lasted a lifetime. We both still thrill at each retelling of our story.

We found our way to a friend's house, tucked at the end of a small dead-end street called Redwood Alley, located on the edge of The Fillmore. The entire alley was inhabited by hippies of the day. It was a ready-made, fluctuating, intense, vital community. And so we began our lives in an environment that expanded our views and options tremendously. Neither of us ever looked back. Luther soon joined his girlfriend who had preceded him, and I took off shortly for Acapulco, a place I had spent much time, only to return to San Francisco in time for the Summer of Love. ("Why are you leaving?" the *lancheros* asked. "I have to find out what the Beatles are doing!" I responded.) That was the summer I hitchhiked from Acapulco to the Pacific Northwest by myself with only $25 in my pocket to cover my costs! That was the summer I learned how protected we are when we have faith. Everything *is* provided; and, experiencing this, the roots of one's spiritual grounding deepen profoundly.

I was particularly blessed to be a part of that culture at that time of my life. I had completed college. I had a head on my shoulders. I did not abuse drugs or alcohol or any of the other substances and situations that were there to lead one off-path. I stayed open, and true to myself, and went on eventually to become a book publicist. This career choice was largely informed by my Sixties values and I have the satisfaction of having made a difference.

As time passed the true San Francisco hippie culture seemed to fade, only to be replaced by unwitting copycats, late arrivers. I will never forget sitting on a public bus that drove through the Haight Ashbury district some years later as the bus driver announced to tourists on the bus that this had been the home to the hippies, but that they were gone. It was like hearing my own obituary.

Forms change. We morph. All of us become rootbound at certain points in our lives and need to be repotted for own growth and expansion. Some of us notice the signs, and consciously choose this for ourselves and others do not heed the calls. Then change may be forced upon us from the outside through deaths, through seeming abandonment, and "lost" jobs. Regardless of how change is delivered to us, each situation holds the seeds of opportunity for growth and expansion. It is always a choice for us how we will hold these events, what we will garner, and whether we will use those junctures for true personal growth and maturity or hold ourselves back through fear, a sense of abandonment, or victimization. Our choice.

CHERISH THE BEAUTY
OF THE SEASON

I must confess that all summer long I have been hovering over a particular canna lily just outside my front door hoping it would blossom before summer's end. Last year it did not have time to come to fruition. This year I have not been disappointed and I take great delight in the spectacular persimmon colored lilies that now grace the entrance to my home.

Three decades ago I was hovering over my own splendid blossom inside my own round tummy. Inside was a precious being getting ready to emerge who was my own beloved Antonia.

Unfettered by any ground outside my front door, I took my round tummy to Acapulco, to stroll and lounge in the sun on the beaches I had come to love in my post-college days. I have always felt so comfortable in Mexico. It is the place of my soul, the culture of my heart, and

Spanish the language of my joy. I have returned over and over again to nurture and restore myself, and to rekindle my faith in humanity, resting in the kindness of the Mexican people and their profound open hospitality. This was the perfect place to be pregnant, in a mother country, in the culture that honors the Divine Mother, whose walls in homes and churches and wayside stations abound with the holy mother. Candles burn to her as a daily part of life. People pray to her. Women are deified, share the holy trinity, are blessed, honored, and included. Yes, this was the place where I wanted my child to grow within me, steeped in the lilting accents heard in the marketplace, in the crashing of blue waves on white sandy beaches, in the glaring sun of the tropics, in the clean air sweeping off the Pacific Ocean into the surrounding parched hillsides. Here is where my Antonia grew.

She drew sustenance from pineapple and mango, papayas and watermelon, and coconuts slathered in lime juice and a bit of cayenne for good measure. Strawberry liquados made with fresh milk. Fish caught fresh from the sea. She grew quietly and slowly, listening to the music of the mariachis who lined the boardwalks each evening. She baked in the sun by day and moved rhythmically inside her mother's womb as her mother joyfully danced with friends by night. We slept late and peacefully, then awoke with nothing, really, to do except to enjoy another day at the beach, another day of being with world travelers, another day of great joy and pleasure and gratitude. Such was her early journey on Earth.

The stage changed as the time of her emergence became imminent. We moved to Mexico City, the place at that time which could provide the modern facilities we needed. We arranged for her to be born in the best hospital in Mexico City.

Two weeks before her "due date" one of my dear friends, Anna from Australia, suggested that we go to hear a friend playing in a band that evening. "There won't be much more time for you to do that," she counseled. Little did we know. I happily agreed and a group of us decided to make the most of the situation and we dressed to the nines. That evening I donned a sheer white smocked long dress, the most feminine of garments, delicately embroidered and fit for a goddess. In this dress I went to town, accompanied by Anna wearing one of my San Francisco frocks I had lent her, a brown velvet and lace dress. All of us were festive and ready for fun and we danced into the night listening to our friend Javier Batiz and his band playing in the Zona Rosa that evening. What fun!

Somewhere during the evening I noticed that I seemed to be having some slight "gas pains". I largely ignored them as they seemed only a moderate discomfort and distraction. Eventually it occurred to me to time the gas pains just to be certain, though I was not due for another two weeks, and I could not imagine my daughter coming early. The gas pains were five minutes apart. Prudence set in and we went home.

I am standing in the kitchen and I am having an enlightened moment.

I am standing in line. It is a very long line. All the folks in line are women. And it is my turn. My body knows exactly what to do. I am awestruck by the immaculate, precise programming and I'm aware suddenly of just how old this is. And I'm simply "next".

We call a taxi. I know it is my job to simply breath. I stay in my breath, knowing that those who love me will get me to the hospital on time. We are driving through the streets of Mexico City in the dead of night in two taxis. The taxi driver is asking someone directions to the American British hospital. I stay in my breath. I'm in an altered state of consciousness. I'm calm and as long as I stay in my breath, centered in my precious breath, I feel no pain.

We are at the hospital. The taxi driver picks me up in his arms and carries me to the door of the hospital. He transfers me to waiting arms at the door and someone says to me, "From this moment on do not use any of your energy." I trust implicitly that I am in the perfect hands. They take care of the outside of my body and I take care of the inside. I am aware that they prep me. No one gives me any drugs.

I am in the delivery room. They say to push. I reach down for my bent legs, putting my hands underneath my thighs, as I had practiced so many times. Someone reaches out to stop me and I say with perfect clarity, from a perfectly centered place, "Yo se lo que estoy haciendo." I know what I'm doing. They respectfully step back.

The doctor says to push. I push three times and out swims my glorious precious girl, my daughter, the most magnificent and most important being in my entire life. My baby girl. My Antonia.

So this is how it went. And they brought her to me swaddled in a light blue blanket, looking perfect. Absolutely beautifully perfect. The most radiant precious lovely skin. The most innocent peaceful blue eyes. Quiet. Perfect. Peaceful. Wondering and aware. And I nursed her and so it began.

What precious season do you cherish most? What beauty that will not linger? What opportunity that you must hold dearest to your heart your whole life through in deepest gratitude, knowing that you have been profoundly touched with one of life's greatest lessons, gifts and blessings? And thusly we cherish the beauty of our seasons.

GENTLY GUIDE THE TENDER VINE,
ELSE IT BECOME WILD,
TANGLED AND IMPOSSIBLE

Show me a fence and I will think of a flower. I will think of honeysuckle, trumpet vine, potato vine, wisteria, jasmine, and morning glories. I will see possibility. I will see beauty. And I will want to get to work right away.

My foray into vines taught me very early on that unless one is paying very close attention they can get away from you. They have minds of their own. You will not be on the same page. At all. You want them to climb over the fence, covering the wires, the boards, the limbs, most likely, and they will want to stretch out their arms in all directions. And, oh, should they touch another surface, be it plant, tree, wall, anything it can expand on, beware. It will take off in the night like a child run wild. And then you have all the undoing to do, to redirect the rampant growth in accordance with your vision. And then you will have some untangling to do. A very gentle, very deliberate, very time consuming, painstaking activity indeed.

We've all done it. We do it in a thousand ways. We were doing this, and then we were doing that, and when we turned our backs for just a moment, or two, things simply got out of control. The mess that ensued was a big fat you know what.

I actually enjoy untangling vines. I do. It reminds me of playing pickup sticks as a child. The slow, calculated act of anticipating what will happen to this when you do that? The ever so gentle unwrapping of this tender tendril from another while keeping it intact, and then the redirection into a creative and pragmatic pattern. It's fun.

The untangling of projects that have gone astray, wayward and awry may not be as engaging, though there are those among us who do enjoy a mess that needs to be straightened out. We enjoy the challenge. What do we do when things have become seemingly unmanageable? The unfailing formula I turn to when I am truly stuck I personally learned from a very wise woman, a professor of mine, author Angeles Arrien. The bottom line version which I have turned to a million times in my mind follows. Any time I find myself faltering, if I run the situation through this four point grid, I will almost always get unglued and be able to view my situation with confidence and clarity.

show up

pay attention

tell the truth

and don't be attached to the outcome

What does this require of me?

Showing up is simply that. I come to the table, fully present.

Paying attention means bringing my full consciousness and heartful-ness in open participation to the process.

Telling the truth means digging down and saying what is true for me, with deep courage and authenticity. My intention is never to hurt another person or myself in this process. It is to get to the bottom of things. The *I Ching* counsels us that a situation cannot change unless and until we are able to face it as it actually is, not as we want it to be. Unless we are willing to do this, the situation will remain in stagnation or deterioration.

Not being attached to the outcome is not easy. It requires a deep sur-rendering. It is an act of faith. It lies in the realm of believing all things happen for a reason, that there is a guiding force at work in our lives that we can trust. This is the essence of being truly grounded in spirit. What are the wild, tangled and impossible tasks and challenges in your life? What do you need to do to resolve them? Do you need assistance or is it something you can do on your own? Will you be stronger and wiser on the other side?

CHERISH THE PRECIOUS VOLUNTEERS

It is curious that flowers that seem to come from nowhere, having no definitive origin, but that spring up in unlikely corners of our gardens are called *volunteers*. It is unlikely I shall ever know the origin of that term but I should like to have known the gardener who thought to call them that, as it is most imaginative. I have always had a special fondness for the volunteers in my various gardens. This year it is a golden dwarf zinnia that stands at attention at the foot of a large bevy of purple echinacea, without a single friend of its own kind to keep it company. But stand it does, no matter. And proud. And lovely.

Some lives are so planned, like our gardens. So fixed. So agreed upon. So unexamined. How does the Universe get through to us when we are on such resolute paths? Perhaps through the uninvited guest or stranger? The person next to us on the plane. In line at the bank. The smiling golden haired child who catches our attention in the market. The canceled plane and the unexpected delay which affords some synchronistic "chance" meeting. A lost job. An unexpected divorce or the death of a dear friend.

Who or what brings these unlikely intrusions into our lives? For what purpose? The zinnia, the random violet or pansy, the California poppy? The one unplanned for, that does not fit our pictures. Be they seeds brought to us by the wind or in the beak of a bird or on the feet of a clambering bumblebee one thing is certain. Each event, each unexpected person, flower, or intuition is all governed by the same unseen hand and force that governs each and every one us. If you are a pragmatist, you can chalk this observation up to the laws that oversee the physical realms that surround you. If you are inclined to reach beyond the obvious into other realms you will find what is often a faint traceline of guidance, of no sheer coincidence, some of which will stack up into some semblance of order, all pointing in some vague but resonant direction. When I see this configuration showing up in my life and opt to choose this path, I happily call this "following the psychic breadcrumbs".

Not every seemingly random occurrence is portent with an urgent life message. It truly is up to us to read and decipher and make sense of what the Universe presents in our path and to choose how we will respond. We do, indeed, have free will within the confines of certain fairly unbending dictums, like, say, gravity. Sometimes we long for guidance and would welcome the stalwart zinnia pointing the way, any way, when we seem to have lost ours. Stay awake. Have faith. Have courage. Find the threads of your life that make up the texture, the warp and weave. Be willing to look in small unobtrusive unlikely places. For each thing, each breath, each moment holds the DNA of the overall plan and you and your life are contained in each stone, each tree, each flower, each mirror that crosses your path. Hold each as a possibility. Some more than others will resonate loudly and clearly. What will you do with what you hold in the gift in your own hand?

ENCOURAGE POTENTIAL

Growing up my mother always insisted that my two sisters and I sing for company. I don't remember her actually teaching me to harmonize, but somehow we did. She taught us old fashioned songs she must have carried with her from Utah to California. Songs like "When It's Springtime in the Rockies" and "You Are My Sunshine" which I sing to this day. For some reason my mother chose rather whimsical nicknames for me and my sisters when we sang and she would call us Agatha Sue, Sarah Jane and Nellie. I was the eldest and I was Agatha Sue.

While my singing roots started by my mother's side, all my young life I sang, mostly in church and school choirs and in college I was in a serious choir that studied things like Mozart's "Requiem" for months on end. I loved the challenge and sophistication of it, just as I had loved Shakespeare since the seventh grade.

By the early 70's I was living with my own daughter in a wonderful old house in Sausalito which overlooked the San Francisco Bay. While living there I happened to hear about a new choir forming at a music school which apparently was housed up at the north end of town on the waterfront out among the houseboats. I decided to check it out. I called and learned that the choir met a certain evening each week. I attended, and next thing I knew I was singing in this lovely large choir of very interesting people. Who held my attention most, however, was our choir director, a small firey woman with long dark curly hair and a powerful voice. I did not learn until years later this woman, Pamela, had gone on tour with some hefty musicians and had recorded her own albums, but I knew she was very good. I was even slightly in awe of her and I was excited to be under her tutelage.

One evening after our rehearsal I lingered, and she approached me, which surprised me, and she said with perfect clarity five magical words, "You have a beautiful voice." The whole inside of my body lit up. I could scarcely believe that this director had singled me out of this large choir and taken the time to acknowledge me. This was a turning point in my perception of my potential as a singer. Someone I admired and looked up to, a role model, had written in big letters across my inner blackboard, "Winner."

It is actually quite awesome to contemplate the power of the spoken word upon the psyche of a budding creative person, but here it was in action. What we tell each other can turn our lives in a New York minute. For better or worse, of course.

I took this spark within me and contemplated it and repeated it to those I trusted. Slowly and tentatively I turned these words over in my mind and I fanned the precious spark to a flame. This lovely woman had taken the torch from the sacred fire and she had passed it along to me. And God bless her.

When my daughter turned five I began to prepare her for a big move. I could not contemplate a life well lived that did not include having resided in Europe. I checked out every book I could find in the library written for children about Europe and I read each one to her at night before she went to sleep. In the fall of that year I flew with her to Paris, where we stayed in a rather posh flat near the Arch de Triumph as the guests of a young French woman who had stayed in our home the previous year. And so began a new and very big chapter in our lives.

After a six-week visit to the south of France I came to the conclusion that I really felt more at home in Holland, which I had visited briefly when we first arrived. We returned to Amsterdam, where my daughter entered a private Dutch school and we settled in. We quickly came to love the Netherlands and the Dutch people.

As fate would have it, among the many people I met in Holland was a local performer. He had a wonderfully rich voice and as friends we began to meet and sing together. I found this very magical. Our voices blended beautifully and I quickly learned all the songs he had written and lent my voice to his harmonically. We knew we had something special. We decided to casually try it out on the public. We heard of a small event taking place at a local church and we arranged to sing for a small informal audience. This was a very new experience for me and I was quite frightened, but I found comfort and strength in my friend's confidence and we were well received. I found the whole process exhilarating!

Our next step was a very big one for me, indeed, and that was to present ourselves to the world as a professional duo, receiving pay for our performance. My singing partner was Dutch, had performed around Holland, and had some good connections. He chose a small inn a couple of hours outside Amsterdam as our first venue. Part of our pay would include lodging at the inn. I felt both nervous and elated with our new venture. I was clearly stepping outside the boundaries of my comfort zone but I drew on the small flame that burned within and the comfort of having someone more experienced to guide the way. The day of our performance arrived. We took the train from the main station in Amsterdam out to the inn and that night I stepped willingly and joyfully on my first stage as a paid performer, one of the thrills of my lifetime. Happily, we were very well received!

After our performance we were shown to the rooms we'd been assigned by the inn. As I entered the small, charming room I had been given for my night's lodging, I glanced around, finding everything quite to my satisfaction, when my eyes lit upon something unusual, something unexpected. An album cover tacked to the wall. I drew towards it to see exactly what it was. There on the wall was Pamela's smiling face beaming out at me on one of her album covers! A flood of emotion washed over me and tears spilled out from my eyes. I smiled back at my friend, there to greet me on the eve of my very first gig on the other side of the Earth.

These are the wonders of life. These are among the small and rich treasures that line the pockets of our deep and abiding memories that we cherish and that bring a smile to our lips and hearts years and years later.

To this day Pamela and I continue to encourage and support each other through the many passages of life. Births, yes, and deaths as well. Always mirroring to each other the best and brightest we know resides within the other, encouraging the holy potential, holding each other's hands and helping each other usher in whatever is next on our paths. And each of us is richly blessed not only with the cherished love of each other but of many such gardeners of our souls, each carefully recognized, and treasured.

To whom do you turn to encourage your dream? Who holds the cleanest mirror, free of projections, of your own emerging best and brightest self? Whom do you trust to have your best interests at heart, who will nurture you to your fullest potential?

BRING GENTLENESS AND GRATITUDE TO YOUR HARVESTING

It happened that while we were living in Amsterdam a small community named Findhorn was garnering headlines in Scotland. Many readers might well be familiar with Peter and Eileen Campbell's story. Peter, a Scottish businessman, and his wife, Eileen, found themselves making an unlikely move to Findhorn, north of Edinburgh, on the Moray Firth, where their inner guidance directed them to begin a garden. The locals smirked behind their backs as the land was quite sandy and arid and salty and farmers were certain Peter was truly daft and delusional to begin to grow anything on such land. But Peter and Eileen were true to their inner directives and began to cultivate many varieties of vegetables and plants. And an extraordinary thing happened. Vegetables and flowers grew beyond what anyone could expect even on good land in the area.

So much so that the Queen of England sent her botanical experts to find out what was occurring at Findhorn. An entire community grew out of that single impulse.

What was occurring at Findhorn began as an internal journey. Eileen and her friend Dorothy Maclean meditated daily for guidance. One of Eileen's keen directives was that it is important to show respect for the plants with which we work. I found this fascinating and began to take this to heart. Eileen counseled that we humbly ask for permission or at least advise a plant if we are to cut off its flowers or pull it up. In light of this, it became ever my practice to extend a grateful energy towards the plant from which I am about to harvest a flower or vegetable or fruit. The times I find myself in a hurry, perhaps just needing a flower here or there to freshen a faltering bouquet, and omitting this simple ritual of respect, I usually catch myself and stop and breathe and begin again. What a difference! The sheer act of extending a conscious gratitude towards the plants that provide me sustenance, medicinal support, and beauty improves the tenor of my own life tenfold. No, a thousandfold! I do not take the plants for granted. I try diligently to hold them in reverence, as I hold all life in reverence. I still pull up weeds, kill bugs (and poisonous snakes) that may cross my path. I do. And I will. But in honoring the common lifeforce that governs us all, regardless of our seeming superiority or inferiority, I add to a body of information, to a lifestyle, to a religiosity that only enhances life on planet Earth for us all.

We are, indeed, all connected. The Bible says, "His eye is on the sparrow, so I know He's watching me." This implies that the Universe's benevolence is extended to all the creatures of the Earth. It would be a travesty to believe that we are any more important in the scheme of things, even if we are different. We all have our place, our contributions, our strengths and weaknesses in the connected web of life, and we rely on each other, species to species, to exist. Extending gratitude, respect, reverence and a gentle countenance towards that which supports us, no matter how seemingly small, is a worthy practice and holds the power to transform the quality of our lives and the days and nights of all who live among us.

PLANT WHATEVER BRINGS YOU JOY!

I had thought I would never live in a city again, having put in time in both San Francisco and Mexico City, but Amsterdam proved to be the exception. It was quite safe, clean, interesting, and charming. Still, after two years passed, I began to grow restless with being in an urban environment. Short trips to the small charming town of Marken broke up the tension of city living, but it was not enough.

In my neighborhood the building of flats across the street had been torn down, leaving a gaping hole as my view. Small trees had been planted at the edge of the broad sidewalks, but we were, when it came down to it, surrounded by cement. My restlessness with the situation grew to agitation. Coupled with the fact we were in an urban environment was the undeniable fact that we were still, after two years, outsiders. By now Antonia spoke fluent Dutch, but she remained somewhat isolated. Her mother was a foreigner. Our neighbors consisted of born-and-bred Dutchmen and a small number of Turkish families (also tagged as forever being foreigners in the eyes of the locals). We were the Americans.

One afternoon I looked out at the brick and concrete landscape, nearly exasperated, and I suddenly heard a voice in me say, "If you don't like it, change it. But don't complain about it anymore." I was startled to hear this voice, but I recognized instantly that it was the truth of the situation.

I went downstairs and examined the sidewalk. Dutch sidewalks are made of very very large (but not deep) cement blocks manufactured elsewhere and then laid down on sand. What I discovered by poking around is that while they are very heavy, they could be removed. A liberating realization! Standing and staring at the broad sidewalk reaching from the wall of our building to the curb, I suddenly envisioned how convenient it would be to remove the blocks just adjacent to the wall. And, once removed, the exposed earth would create a perfect sized garden plot! Interesting!

I advised my landlord, who lived downstairs, what I intended to do. No protest from him. I enlisted the help of a couple of male friends, and they were able to pry up four of the large cement blocks in front of our building and move them to the area behind our flat (just in case the City Fathers ever wanted them put back). I dug up the sand underneath to a depth of about two feet. Perfect. Antonia and I filled up the hole I had made with fresh earth. I began to purchase flowering plants and gradually filled the earthen area with their living beauty.

And a strange thing happened. Strangers began appearing at the door of my flat. Strangers who had previously shied away from us "foreigners". Some brought plants. And some shoved money into my hands! I was dumbfounded, amazed and delighted!

Children showed up to help set the plants in the ground. Soon we had our garden! We had made a difference in our neighborhood. Everyone could see and enjoy the beauty. It made my heart burst with joy. The momentum from that single action was so unexpected.

One evening an elderly woman came to the door and told me she lived down the street and that her husband was an invalid who sat inside all day. Watching out the window was one of his main activities. She asked humbly if we would consider coming down to their flat and planting another garden, which we did.

This simple act of the willingness to go against the grain, to step outside the box, to challenge the way things had always been done proved to be a deeply transformational experience for both me and my daughter, and the heartstrings that surrounded this vision and action extended into the hearts and minds and eyes of a neighborhood.

What seeds of joy might you plant that would transform your life and those around you? What commitment would it take? What risk? What courage? What vision have you discounted as impossible? What would you gain by doing something about it and what might you lose by not?

ROTATE YOUR CROPS

Every good farmer knows that you can't keep growing the same darn thing in a field. It'll wear it out. Why are we any different? While there is something to be said for having a plan, developing a talent, keeping a focus and reaching for success, there is also something to be said about getting in a rut and burning out.

We need variety. Different tasks bring out different talents, different skills. Again, a cautionary here. I am not advocating taking a person who does well at his job and because of that moving him up the ranks as a "reward" into something he's not suited for. No. I'm talking about developing new skills, adding something different, trying something new, taking a risk. I rewrote a Browning quote to suit my gender and it's permanently on my desk. Scribbled on a post-it it says, "A woman's reach should exceed her grasp."

I've done a lot of different things. Worked a lot of jobs to make a living, keep a roof over my head, pay the bills. I've also lived in four different countries for lengthy periods of time and I speak two languages and have a small grip on two or three more.

Probably one of the more interesting work adventures I had was helping a group of international folks open and run a vegetarian restaurant on the Museumplein in Amsterdam. I think the picture conjured when one thinks of running a restaurant in this country is about as stressful a job as one can imagine. And not really that glamorous or interesting. It sounds like really hard work. And probably not that fun. Right?

The restaurant we began, called (interestingly) The Garden, did not follow any of the traditional roles or rules about running a restaurant. The owner, Han, was creating a remarkable little experiment. Apparently he had read the book *Small is Beautiful*, and while I honestly have never read the book, this was his bible, on which he told us the business was founded. Whatever the precepts were, and I imagine he took great license, this is what he did.

First of all he apparently decided to hire mostly foreign travelers to run the restaurant. We were from Chile, from Israel, America, Argentina, from France, England, Germany, Belgium, and India. There was one Dutch person I can recall and he was half Indonesian. When you get this many people from different countries you get several languages. At any given time one could hear at least three languages being spoken, simultaneously in the kitchen, by the same people, as most of us were at least bilingual.

Secondly, while we did not pay the bills, we ran the restaurant. That's how Han set it up.

We had Monday Morning Meetings. We gathered together every Monday morning and we processed any issues (also unusual), and then we set up the schedule for the week. We had a calendar that illuminated all the shifts and jobs that had to be filled during the week. Here were the rules. We could work as many shifts as we wanted (one or twelve—or not at all!) and we could work any job we wanted. As long as all the shifts for all the jobs were filled, that was fine. Who does that?? This was an enormously liberating structure within which to work that certainly accommodated the needs and desires of a crew of folks who were basically world travelers. And it worked. All the jobs were always filled and everyone was always happy. What a concept!

Here was another rule. If you worked there, you could eat there. Anytime. And we did. So food was part of the deal, also very attractive to traveling people on fairly fixed budgets.

Another interesting rule. While there was a "bakery staff" (who came in early before the cook of the day needed the small kitchen) who made some regular items (vegetarian pie, taught to us by a charming and quirky woman from northern England; banana cream pie, and Power Cake, a recipe brought by a Dutch woman from The Farm in Tennessee), we served only one meal a day. Whatever was written on the chalkboard menu nailed to the wall was what was being served that day. Whoever cooked that day decided what was being made that day. And, the decision was based on what the cook for that day found in the cupboard and refrigerator. So we never knew. It was always a surprise (even to the person who came in that morning to cook!). And it was always different. And it always worked.

And business thrived. People lined up every day for those home-cooked creative healthy meals.

I can't quite imagine that this would "work" in America. Or let's say this. The way we do business does not lend itself to this kind of experiment. There is something non-challenging about the Dutch. Some say it's because there are no natural borders, no hills or mountains or rivers to keep invaders out. Maybe. But one would have to say that the Dutch are an extremely tolerant bunch, very accepting of different lifestyles. Again, I would plead that this is another way of rotating your crops: do business in another country. Explore other cultures. Learn how other people live.

There is much to be said for patriotism. I'm sure. I deeply appreciate the freedoms we have here. But there are other cultures, other ways of living just as valid, trust me on this. Beauties of other languages. Beauties in other skins, other religions, other ways of being. It is simply myopic to think that God created one special way of being, one religion, one skin color He/She favored. And what? The rest of humanity is doomed? In the centered quiet of one's heart, in the deepest recesses of your mind, surely it is not that big a stretch to understand, to embrace that God created all living beings under a plan. It is our diversity that frightens us. It is our Unity that frightens us more, however.

I remember that not long after I moved to Holland I stepped inside a cafe one night, and I looked around the room and I watched my mind think the following horrific thought (true confessions), "You mean all these people aren't Americans and it's all right?" I stopped short and could not believe I had just thought that. In a flood and flash of realization I became aware that I'd been brought up believing that American was not only the best to be, it was the only thing to be, and that everyone else was, what? Lacking? Wrong? Unfortunate? I am here to tell you, that is not true.

I can't think of a single thing that would perpetuate world peace more than living elsewhere for awhile. If you really think you can't do that, send your children, and let them experience another culture, another language. Our geography isolates us terribly. Our media is sorely lacking in international coverage. We wear blinders largely placed upon us by someone else, some agreement we never realized has been made. Until we fully open our hearts to understand and embrace that there are many peoples (and species) on the planet Earth (that's with a capital "E"), that we have limited resources, that we share one living resource, and that that resource is threatened, we live in an illusion.

Rotate your crops.

HONOR THE SEED PLANTED
BY ANOTHER HAND

For who knows exactly what reason I come from a rather nomadic family. My paternal roots are sunk deeply into 17th C. New England culture, so I have to think this comes from my maternal family, knowing that my maternal great-grandmother made her way as a very young woman across the great Atlantic alone on a ship, having left Norway to find a new life in America. Stories passed down about her include the observation, "She liked to move a lot," and mortgage records indicate this was true. My grandmother subsequently moved a lot, my mother moved a lot, I have moved a lot (and now my daughter moves a lot). Anyone who knows me at all will substantiate this story. One thing I have cherished in moving from place to place is my encounter with a wide variety of gardens. I have deeply relished the experience of walking through what is now "my new garden" and seeing what is there, perhaps among the weeds and brush, that gradually I have cleared away, revealing a lily here, an iris there, old rose bushes, trumpet vine and myrtle, always expanding my knowledge as I go. I love the process of discovery, and of restoring the beauty that once was. However one of the things I treasure most in this process is the invisible thread I feel spun that connects me to the woman (most likely) or man who planted that living thing to start with. I feel in my heart the connection I make with that unknown gardener, the gratitude and wonder and curiosity I always feel towards that creative person, pondering the original intention, and the place I now take as I move forward on that original impulse towards beauty. Who knows where that gardener might be today? That person easily might not even be here on Earth, but that impulse, the vision, is alive and being nurtured and brought forth, even if the gardener is gone. I love that thought. Then I imagine what it might mean for our society, to the family of man, if each of us, as we come in contact with all of life were to think upon what the original impulse must have been and what responsibility we bear to what and whom we find before us. Do we nurture, weed, ignore, cherish or benefit, reaping the promise inherent in the opportunity? Do we even notice? What gardens lie before us unharvested, untended? What is the connection with the past and our present? Does it matter? Is there any obligation to someone else's future? What seeds are we planting, tending, nurturing and leaving for the next hand to come later? I cannot help but think of the ever so precious giant redwood trees of California so threatened by greed and unconsciousness. Or of the ancient diminishing rainforests that hold their invaluable secret healing medicines provided to us by our Creator being lost on an hourly basis in the name of "progress". Or of our air, our waters, our Earth and of the women and men and children who will inherit the fruits of our actions, of our consciousness, of our thoughtfulness or lack thereof.

NEVER UNDERESTIMATE THE
POWER OF ONE TINY SEED

For anyone needing a prescription for faith and wonder I heartily recommend the following. Go to a nursery and buy a package of lobelia seeds. Any variety will do. Come home and *very* carefully open the package. (Make sure no breeze is blowing!) Look inside. Pour the seeds out in your hand and contemplate their minute size and then look at the picture on the front of the package. If you are not sufficiently moved, get some dirt, put it in a container, stick some seeds somewhere close to the top layer, place the container in the sun and water gently for ten days. As the delicate green begins to emerge and happy faced tiny purple and blue and white flowers begin to blossom allow yourself to contemplate the fact that the same forces of nature that govern the teeny lobelia seed govern *you*. Lobelia seeds, not unlike many others, are so small they would at first glance appear to have no value whatsoever! How could anything that tiny turn into anything anyone might be interested in? Yet given the right environ and nurturance the tiny seed grows to a hearty colorful plant that borders gardens and livens planters worldwide. If you were given the right sustenance, the corresponding water, earth, light and food, what might you become? There really is no difference. Anytime you forget your own value and worth, consider the size of the little lobelia seed and remember that you, yourself, contain a seed within that longs to come to fruition. That is what you are here for. That is your task and your destiny. What might you yield, dearest readers, under the right conditions? Take yourself there!

NURTURE, NURTURE, NURTURE

Near as I can tell life on planet Earth is mostly about taking care. Taking care of our families. Taking care of our friends. Taking care of the work that we take responsibility for. Taking care of our homes, taking care of our possessions, our animals, our gardens, our plants, our cars, our water, our air, our land. Our churches, our communities, our cities, our roads, our poor, our sick, our wounded, our frail and elderly. Taking care of ourselves. Taking care of ourselves physically. Taking care of ourselves mentally. Taking care of ourselves emotionally. And taking care of ourselves spiritually. Yep, I'd say that pretty much covers life on our planet for we human beings, and it certainly reflects my experience!

Now how we go about that is endless in its possibilities. As varied as the fish in the sea, the birds in the sky, the plants in the forest. And notice they are all taking care as well.

If I ask myself what is the central principle behind this endless and perpetual taking care, I'd have to say life itself. Life reaching towards life. Life ensuring life continues. That essentially is the drive behind it all, is it not? Each and every living thing on planet Earth is hardwired for doing well, for keeping the whole thing going, for perpetuating life. The lengths various species go to ensure their sticking around boggles the mind.

As we are caught up in our own individual dramas and the illusions (and grandeurs) of our sense of separation, it is easy (and convenient) to forget what the essential driving force behind all this is. Truly there are beings walking planet Earth thinking it was about them. "What? It's not about me?" Well, it is. You and over six billion other people and a several billion other species. It is humbling to contemplate when we take the time.

And the distorted ways in which some of us choose to take care of ourselves and others are absolute abominations, there is no doubt. But often underneath the aberration one could find this slender thread of life's longing at the core, hard as that might seem.

What would our lives look like if we consciously brought the value of taking care, of nurturing to the fore. How would aligning ourselves with that single focus impact our lives and the lives of others? If we acknowledged fully our intrinsic programming to care and nurture for all that came within our view, our path, our neighborhood, our own small radar, what impact would that accumulative shift have on our larger reality?

Jesus said to love one another. Was that not the same?

WEAR THE RIGHT GARB

Decorating one's home, office *and* oneself are all ways of honoring the spirit of the season, usually dating back to some very old tradition that ties more to the plantings of spring, the bounty of summer and fall and the sequestering demands of winter than we would ever imagine. We readily draw from nature in our festive endeavors. We gather bouquets of blossoms from the generous offerings of our gardens and place them in lovely vases about our homes to mark important holidays and passages. We harvest grapevines and cattails and wheat and bittersweet in fall and fashion them into wreathes we hang upon our doors, welcoming guests who draw together before the cold of winter isolates us one from the other. We chop wood that we burn in our hearths to keep the bitter cold at bay. Though we often lose sight of it, we are not only inextricably tied to the seasons of nature, we are a part of it.

It is a charming observation that plants always know what to wear, no matter what the season. In spring and summer roses are beautifully appointed. They give us pleasure, lift our spirits, and offer their exquisite fragrance and beauty. Daises are more rough and tumble, and seem to draw a smile. The dainty columbine offers us a bit of old-fashioned subtle charm. Each flower, bush, tree and bud knows its place in the scheme of things and dresses accordingly.

I am the kind of woman who wears orange and black on Halloween, red and green on Christmas and something pastel (and probably floral) on Easter. I just am.

Painted in my childhood memories are a dark, rich burgundy velvet dress with a rounded white lace collar. This dress is etched forever in my Christmas memory book. As a teen I remember the absolutely visceral thrill of deciding to wear a small red hat with a lavender dress and coat and high heels on Easter Sunday, making an early bold statement about my independent nature. Or borrowing my mother's cashmere sweaters, luscious butterscotch and pale blue and wearing them to high school classes. I fondly recall a bold houndstooth black and white wool checkered coat that sheltered me from the winter snows. I am all of this and more.

Are we so unlike the flowers?

Are you the elegant rose, the sturdy daisy, the tumbling tumbleweed rolling across dusty plains? Are you the shy mountain iris, the chrysanthemums of Thanksgiving, or December's holly or ivy? The burning bush of Appalachia, the traditional hydrangea, beautiful though faded, or the steady and reliable geranium, tucked on a winter's ledge next to a white lace curtain on this side of the glass, looking out? Or do you venture forth with the showy blaze of a bird of paradise?

What is it you turn to mark the special passages of time with those you love? What gay and festive treasures? What fancy flights of expressions of who you really are?

AIM FOR BEAUTY

Three years after arriving in Holland we returned to the States and I began my fledgling publicity business. I took a couple of offices in the county seat of Marin Co. in Northern California and put up a sign announcing my intentions. My two offices were at the back of a building on the main drag of the downtown. There was a metal stairwell at the back end of the hall, for fire safety primarily, that led into a small and bare concrete courtyard, fenced in by hurricane fencing, and a small private parking area lay outside the fence. I would look out through my back window into this barren area and cringe when on occasion a local vagrant person would find a place to sit outside the fence nursing something in a paper bag. This situation was not savory or attractive. What could I do?

I descended the fire staircase into the courtyard and surveyed it carefully. Weeds jutted randomly in cracks in the cement. Clearly there was not much to work with, but surely I could do something. Right?

I stepped through the heavy metal gate into the small parking lot outside and poked futilely with my finger in the narrow margin of dirt along the fenceline that had somehow escaped being covered with blacktop and a teeny spark of hope and imagination kindled. A little smile crept across my lips as I began to think of seeds.

Inspired, I went to the nursery and purchased morning glory seeds. I developed a deep and abiding fondness for blue morning glories which used to climb up on my deck when I lived for many years in Sausalito, facing the San Francisco Bay. Who would not appreciate their charming beauty and abundance? Suddenly I was envisioning a wall of morning glories covering that back fence, creating a screen from the commercial lot into which I looked and thinking what a boon (and surprise!) it would be for anyone whose steps crossed that area.

Excited, I brought the seeds home and soon was out there poking around with a gardening tool on the outside of the fence, in that narrow ridge of hope. I pushed in the trowel. Thump. What was that? You might imagine the deflating impact it had on me when I realized that just under a couple of inches of dirt was the extended dreaded blacktop. I was crushed, and I cursed a society that covered up every inch of possibility with asphalt.

The next morning I gazed dejectedly out the small office window at the wretched fence and courtyard and relayed my story to a friend on the phone.

"Yes. That's right. Blacktop. Do you believe it? And I was so excited. My morning glories would have been so pretty. And the only thing I can think of is to find someone with a jackhammer to get through that stuff, unlikely as that is. I can't do it on my own."

Just at that very moment my gaze moved a little further beyond the fence to the opposite side of the private parking lot. Along the edge of the lot were four men, four *strong* men doing some kind of repair work—with jackhammers!

Immediately my spirits soared as I realized the opportunity that the Universe was placing directly before me!

"Justine? I have to go. You won't believe this, but there are a bunch of guys out there working on the lot with jackhammers!"

I flung open the back door and rushed down the stairs, all smiles. I knew without a doubt they were my heroes!

I approached one of the men, smiling.

"Hi! Is your boss here?"

"My boss?" the man answered, confused.

"Yeah, your boss. Is he here by any chance?"

The man indicated a man off to the side, whom I had not seen, and I immediately moved toward him, grinning.

"Hi. I know this is going to sound crazy, but do you have a minute? Can I show you something?"

Reluctantly the man followed me to the fence. I poured out my story with all the passion I felt.

"See?" I concluded, poking my finger in the ground and looking up at him imploringly. "Is there any possibility your men could open this up for me? Just an inch here and there? Just enough to get in a seed? Please?"

The blessed man heard my plea. To my utter delight, without another word to me he walked back to his crew and spoke with the men, pointing in my direction. I was thrilled! I went back upstairs to ring Justine and tell her of my good fortune, watching the men from the window with their marvelous jackhammers, opening up the field of possibility and hope. I was witnessing a miracle for which I gave hearty thanks and I ran back down and beamed at the men with appreciation as they obligingly dug my holes. Five minutes of work; a summer's pleasure.

Over the next weeks my morning glories sprouted and wound their faithful way up the cyclone fence, lending inch by inch the grace of their steadfast beauty. I fussed over them daily, training their tendrils upward. I took the greatest pleasure in beginning my workday out there within my new and unexpected garden, taking note of any new growth, as I sprayed a gentle stream of glistening water onto their lovely emerging faces.

Spring into summer I would grin and nod at passersby who witnessed the slow and steady transformation, acknowledging with them "what a difference it was going to make". By summer's end the sweet morning glories bursting from their lovely green vines had fully covered the cyclone fence from one end to the other. Their precious splendor spilled over the top and back down again, filling in the vapid unimaginative space of practicality with the blessing promised in a bit of creativity, determination and the goodheartedness of a few good men willing to indulge in a vision.

Dear ones, regardless of your situation, aim for beauty.

TAKE COMFORT IN THE MYSTERY

Simultaneous with building my publicity business I became aware
that Antonia needed to be in a private school. Indeed, I had heard
those very words in my head, as a clear directive, the kind you do not
ignore. "Antonia belongs in a private school." So I was not terribly surprised when my path led me spontaneously and synchronistically to a
Christmas event at a local Rudolf Steiner School. Within a month the
Cosmic Plan unfolded and I found myself teaching Spanish classes at
the school which qualified Antonia to attend, as the child of faculty. All
of my students at the school were very special to me. And one of these
very special students was a young, dark, earthy girl named Cara, who
was about six years old. She had a rather round face, dark brown eyes,
and very smooth perfect skin. Unfortunately, I learned that beneath that
perfect skin coursed blood that was not in a state of balance. Cara had

leukemia. This was shocking to learn. One does not usually think that a small child building a body and moving into life is threatened so soon in losing it. Such a situation informs us that we must move into the realm of trust and acceptance and living each moment as fully as one can with the life we are given together.

Cara was blessed to have very loving parents. They lived in a lovely home on the ocean's edge, and this is where Cara spent the remaining days of her life, out near the beautiful Pacific Ocean. I heard that shortly before she passed she was holding in her arms (and heart) the newborn baby of her teacher from school, and this somehow gave us all some comfort in knowing this, her last story.

Shortly after Cara crossed over her parents called me unexpectedly and asked me if I would sing at her funeral. They knew that singing songs in class was something I often did, and that apparently Cara enjoyed. I was taken off guard, but of course I accepted the request as an honor. I knew almost immediately that I could not find a song for this occasion but I would have to create one for this little girl, something I had never done before.

One day shortly after, as I was getting on the freeway on my way to a business meeting, suddenly and completely unexpectedly, an entire song entered my mind intact. This had never happened before and it has not happened since. I arrived at the meeting excited and needing to write it down, which I did.

Days later I found myself driving out to the coast on a foggy morning, winding my way down that lovely two lane stretch of Pacific coast highway in Marin County, through the woods, looking closely for a small cemetery that lay along the highway's edge, marked by a white picket fence. There people were gathered to mark and celebrate Cara's young life. Here is the song I was given for Cara, and which I sang for her on that foggy morning, in the company of those who loved her:

Cara's Song
At last my eyes are open
And I see what I've always known
That every star in the morning sky
Is an angel calling me home

Calling me home again
Calling me home again
Calling me home again
Calling me home.

At last my eyes are open
And I see what I've always known
That every wave of the ocean
Is an angel calling me home

Chorus

At last my eyes are open
And I see what I've always known
That every deer on the meadow
Is an angel calling me home

Chorus

At last my eyes are open
And I see what I've always known
That every smile in a baby's eye
Is an angel calling me home

Chorus

I cannot explain how this song came to me. I take deep comfort in
the mystery of not knowing.

NEVER PULL UP AND DISCARD
WHAT YOU CANNOT IDENTIFY

One morning while I was living in Marin County, I received a phone call from the girlfriend of a man I knew, though I hardly knew the woman. Indeed, I thought it was strange she had called me. She explained that she had agreed to greet people at a workshop/luncheon being held at a nearby restaurant, to receive their payments, and to give them namecards, but that she was unable to keep this commitment and she wondered if I might go in her place. This was not something I would ordinarily do. And somehow I was slightly annoyed she had called me, almost a stranger, to ask me to fill in for her. I'm sure I told her I had to think about it. Then I could not think of a single reason, really, why I could not, and so I agreed. Still, there was a small amount of tension within me that I would be taking time to be helping her out with what I clearly thought was a somewhat unusual activity.

I arrived at the small restaurant and the task was simple. Extend myself to those arriving, and make sure everything was in order.

I learned there was to be a Native American woman, a teacher, speaking at the luncheon. I had had no exposure to Native American teachings and had never been inclined in that direction, but I was there and could see the advantage of being present and open and following along for the journey. Journey, indeed.

The teacher's name was Leslie Gray. She seemed quite sophisticated and well educated and not what I was expecting, in the little time I'd had to form any kind of impression. She was a smallish, strong and direct woman with very dark hair. She was carrying a flat drum. She told us she was going to introduce us to a process called "a journey." She asked us to close our eyes and she began to beat this large round flat drum in an even round rhythm and she began to guide us verbally into a new experience. Being familiar with guided meditation I was used to following the directives of a person leading such an exercise, but I had never had the experience of being guided with a drum.

Leslie told us to watch for a hole in the ground, not unlike the holes, say, garden chipmunks dive into, but larger. A tunnel. I did, indeed, see a tunnel, and I followed Leslie's words and entered the tunnel, not knowing where it would lead. At this point what ensued internally was the equivalent of watching a very vibrant colorful film in which I was a character. I found myself emerging on flat desert terrain, with a tree to my left and mountains in the distance, and a Native American woman wrapped in a colorful long blanket of ochre and reds and blacks to my right. She seemed very traditional, wise and older. She had long dark hair, tied back and she spoke to me. She said one thing only. She said, "You should be studying with Leslie Gray." I was shocked.

Moments later Leslie was directing us to emerge from the altered state we had been in (all to varying degrees, I'm sure) by coming back up through the tunnel which we had entered at the beginning of the exercise. I opened my eyes to the light of the Mill Valley restaurant, kind of bleary eyed and wondering. The luncheon was over shortly thereafter and I returned home, thinking about my experience, and not quite sure what to do with the information the Native American woman had given to me.

Having mulled her words over for a couple of days I decided to call Leslie Gray in San Francisco. I simply told her what the woman in my journey had told me. Leslie said that she taught at a graduate school in San Francisco in the anthropology department. I had had no intention of entering graduate school at the time. I was a single parent, running my publicity business and adding anything to my schedule or responsibilities was the furthest thing from my mind. This was not anything I had budgeted for and I told her so, and we ended the conversation.

Two days later Leslie called me back and she said, "You know what? Call the head of the department. The last thing she said to me was that she wanted to promote the program."

I called the head of the department and told her what had ensued that led to my contacting her. Her response was, "I have just returned from India. This is the first call I have taken. The foremost thing on my mind is promotion for my program. Come in and talk."

This is how I entered graduate school, studying social and cultural anthropology. It had never been my conscious intention. This turn in the road—initiated by a phone call asking me for a favor that had initially annoyed me—led not only to my furthering my education with some of the most incredible teachers I had ever had, but also to a completely different direction in the kinds of books I was promoting, through unexpected, new contacts I made at the school. I felt as if God had tapped me on the shoulder and said to me, "Your work with the kinds of books you have been promoting is now complete. Now it is your task to begin to promote business books that will help transform the workplace."

Thinking back, I wonder what would have happened if I had declined this woman's request? What if I had not taken the time to at least consider? Sometimes opportunities for change and transformation come wrapped in the most unlikely of packages, some which might even grate on our nerves or perplex us.

There is a plant I have been watching warily most of summer in my garden. With the roughest of large unsightly of leaves, it looked every bit like a weed. Finally, at the very end of the season, it has blossomed into some odd sort of rudbeckia with large yellow flowers bringing lovely bright color to a declining garden rushing into fall. All summer I threatened to pull it up, not knowing what it was, but did not, as I was determined to live by my own precepts. I'm glad I did!

RECOGNIZE WHEN A PLANT'S LIFE IS
SPENT AND BE WILLING TO LET IT GO

On my forty-seventh birthday at ten to five in the afternoon I went to a pound in a little town on the coast of Mendocino County to look for a dog. This was no ordinary pound. It was begun by a retired vet who had moved out to the coast and found the situation governing stray animals lacking. So on this sunny afternoon what I found were five dogs tied to a chainlink fence under some trees. As I walked tentatively and somewhat ambivalently from dog to dog, a small black Border Collie unexpectedly sat on her haunches and placed her front feet ever so gently on my knees, looking up at me, asking. In the eleven years I was blessed to have this dog, Moxie, I never saw her do this again. And it did work. Still, I have to admit I was not immediately smitten. The young girl in charge that day offered the old, "Take her home and if you don't like her, you can bring her back." So I took her home.

We went for walks in the woods. I gave her a bath. I massaged her and worked with smoothing out her energy. And as she began to relax, a bond was formed, the likes of which I had never experienced with any animal. She was so intelligent and sensitive. I remember the first time I suddenly awoke in the middle of the night and she was sitting motionless beside me, staring directly at me. Her sheer energy had awakened me. She wanted out.

As fate would have it, my next door neighbor had a Border Collie and soon I was learning about this particular breed, going to dog shows to watch these extraordinary animals herding sheep and I began to understand what I had brought into my life, including the power of the the Border Collie's stare! They use it to move sheep where they want them to be! (She could herd me in my sleep!)

We began her training in earnest on a beach on a small river where it joined the ocean. I would put her in a seated position, raise my hand to indicate she was to stay and I would walk several hundred yards further up the beach and then open my arms wide to indicate she was to come to me, and she would rush headlong towards me, delighted with the game and ever so proud of her accomplishments. She was extraordinary. She was playful. She was kind. She was loving. She was protective and watchful and mindful. And she had my back, always. If we ever had to drive home after dark she would sit in the passenger seat and watch the road with intention. When we lived in the woods and I, on occasion, had to go out into the dark of night to accomplish some task left undone, she went with me. I always found her companion energy to be supportive and a real force to be drawn from. I did better when she was there, and she was always there. I took her almost everywhere. We were virtually inseparable. We were true companions. She helped me live my life.

She was also an escape artist. This dog was virtually impossible to contain. Once, she got out of a backyard fence and I searched high and low in exasperation, looking for how she did it. I could find no holes. I finally put her up against the fence line and stood on the outside of the fence with an open can of tuna fish, demanding that she show me how she got out. After five minutes of intense insisting, she finally and reluctantly moved skillfully through the fence itself. This required her to contract her body into a space that allowed her to move through a square in the wire that was six inches square, at most. Even though I watched her do it, I could not believe my eyes.

She was a clever one, that girl, and always retained a mind of her own. Her idea of a good time alone was to carouse in the woods sniffing anything and everything, to chase squirrels up into large pine trees and bark at them incessantly and then, to finish off a perfectly good escape day, to roll in the most obnoxious thing she could find, preferably something dead.

She had a penchant for being the bullseye target for skunks and many a night I gave that girl a tomato juice bath, scolding her in the bathtub at 2:00AM, after she'd gone out for a little middle of the night pee. She got foxtails up her nose that vets meticulously removed for a hundred bucks. Doggie stuff.

Eventually we added another Border Collie, Peaches, to our clan, and I was the alpha doggie of my pack. Oh, the adventures we went on, the places we saw, the things we did. We were a glorious tribe, the center of a life that held space for chickens, cats, canaries and all manner of things that crossed our paths as we moved nomadically around Northern California, savoring the various lifestyles that were abundantly, richly to be found. The ocean. Wine country. The valleys of Marin. Inland. We did it all. We happily adapted and found new treasures and pleasures in each new spot. We spent hours playing frisbee and ball. They kept me company in the garden. They slept under my computer desk when I worked, waiting patiently for our outdoor time. We were good friends.

Then something happened. Moxie simply wasn't well. Her illness came very unexpectedly and followed closely on the heels of a series of losses, including the death of my 100 year old Grandmother, who had simply aimed herself at heaven and willed herself off the planet Earth.

It was her time. That one I had expected. I had not expected Moxie's time with us to be so short.

I took her to a Northern California veterinary school for a second opinion. There was no way around it. Moxie was leaving our clan. And the hardest part of all was that I was going to have to initiate the passing. I resisted until we sat quietly one sunny afternoon together in the apple orchard where we had shared so many pleasant days. She was sitting closely by my feet. "Does it hurt?" I asked. She turned her head deliberately and looked into my eyes with pain and sorrow. "Thank you for telling me the truth," I told her and tears brimmed as I knew now what I was going to have to do.

Over the next ten days on three occasions I drove her up the coast to that lovely sand beach where I had first trained her. Her energy was flagging. She would sit quietly on the beach and take it in. The last time I took her up there we walked slowly out to the ocean's edge and she unexpectedly stepped into deep water, something she never did. She walked deliberately in the cold sea's gently lapping waves and looked back over her shoulder directly at me three times. She knew.

We chose a time. My vet came to my home and in an instant lying in the comfort of her own garden, Moxie left. I was shocked at how fast it went. She was cremated and her ashes remain with us in a small urn. I know for a fact this dog is waiting for me on the other side. I know she will be there at the end of that tunnel of light waiting to greet me and we will continue our journey in whatever form that takes.

Not long ago I was watching tv and someone was doing a controlled scientific study on psychics. The study consisted of having several psychics interview a series of individuals separately to see if there was any correlation between the data they picked up. I sat and wept as I watched one particular woman go through a series of three different sessions with three different psychics and each one said to her, "There seems to be a little dog trying to get through to you. Did you have a dog? A little dog? She's barking and barking and wants you to know she's there."

Yes, I did. My Moxie. She was one of my teachers. I learned from her that when a life is spent one must recognize that fact and be willing to lovingly let it go.

USE THE RIGHT TOOL FOR THE JOB

The *I Ching* cautions that there is always something one sided about the learning of the self taught. When it came to gardening, in the beginning, I was pretty much self taught. As I grew up no plant was truly safe in my mother's care, sadly true. And while my grandmother managed to do stunningly with a small clip of ivy someone smuggled back for her from Buckingham Palace it would be safe to say these were not skills I learned at home at anyone's knee. Thus it would not be uncommon to find me squatting in the garden in a robe early mornings digging a hole with, oh, say, a spoon. So it was my great good fortune when I moved into a house out in San Geronimo Valley that came with a gardener. His name was Fernando, and he was from Brazil. As it so happened Fernando was studying horticulture in a local college. Lucky me. He would arrive early mornings with two or three Mexicans in tow and we would all get to work. Oh, I followed them around like a puppy and learned everything I could from them. I pitched right in. I loved having their help and I loved that they taught me about tools and how to do things properly. ("All those muscles rippling on your behalf, " my friend Mary used to grin.) One of the things Fernando used to tell me is that it is better to dig a five dollar hole for a one dollar plant than a one dollar hole for a five dollar plant. This, by nature, would mean one would have to give up spoons. So I began to buy tools. I discovered that one of the reasons men could do things I could not was that they had the right tools for the job. This was an enlightening moment for me and this lesson continues to reverberate through my experience to this day. There are nuances to shovels. Flat headed shovels do things pointy ones can't. It is better to use a spackle knife than butter knives or spatulas for plastering holes. There are tools specifically designed to dig up weeds with sharp fingers called hand held hoes, so one needn't pull on weeds endlessly, ruining one's fingers and nails. Which brings up gloves. It was such a turning point for me to discover leather gloves. How many rose bushes had I pruned, or wild blackberry bushes had I pulled out without the benefit of the protection of leather gloves? And the day I discovered tree lopping shears, I went wild in the garden with my new found power, lamenting all the time I'd tried to do the same job with hedge shears. And then I graduated to some power tools, which are heaven. So this really has been a happenstance love affair in the garden, always discovering something new that makes my journey easier.

One day I discovered the joys of cement. It just fascinates me what you can put together, the realms you can move into creatively with the benefit of cement. Cement and the help of my gardeners, I should say. Often I find I can conceive of something I want to build, but I need guidance and support to actually make it. Two such projects were the two sidewalks I created on my property in Santa Rosa which I found very thrilling. I started out at my favorite local building supply store consulting with their project people who are very patient and helpful. They listened to what I wanted to build and they told me exactly what I needed for the job. They even helped me measure things out specifically. I deeply valued the input of these people who were well placed in their positions both in skill and temperament, who guided me patiently into creative realms I felt passionate about but needed guidance to get there.

I called my Mexican gardeners, both from Michoacan, whose people are very in touch with the land. They came and showed me how to prepare the areas where I wanted the sidewalks, how to dig and fill and flatten the sand, how to lay down materials that deterred weeds and finally how to lay down the large bricks I had chosen into a lovely pattern. Each step required specific tools without which the task would have been very difficult. Their knowledge and skills and strength were all part of requisite success of what I wanted to accomplish. I finished off the project by scratching in the day's date into a fresh cement square at the beginning of the new sidewalk to the guesthouse, for posterity. This was enormously gratifying.

In what areas of your life are you still using a spoon to dig five dollar holes? Where in your life are you trying to do everything when you truly need some muscle rippling on your behalf? And what new fun things could you do if you used the right tools for the job?

RESIST THE TEMPTATION TO PLANT
MORE THAN YOU CAN CARE FOR

You'd think I would have learned this lesson the summer I zealously planted an entire package of zucchini seeds and they all came up. We had a running counting chart on the frig and we harvested well over a hundred zucchinis (which we donated to a local food bank). Who knew?

This was different. And it seemed so innocent. A canary. OK, a canary and his girlfriend. The males sing, right? With the first girlfriend, that's how it appeared. Two canaries in a cage. Fernando (yes, named after my dear gardener!) and Bianca. What could go wrong? And Fernando had a happy song that filled the house and all was well. For months, really.

One sad morning I found the little body of Bianca on the floor of the cage. Oh, dear. An appropriate funeral followed in the garden. Tears were shed, and then, of course I had to go get another girlfriend for Fernando.

You can't just have one of anything. It's not fair to a species. So Felicity came home to live with us. As it happened, this canary was not at all like Bianca. For one thing she really liked to build nests. And she was very good at it. Innovative, in fact. She built them in the water dish, in the seed cup, in anything she could find she could sit in (or thought she could). Building materials? No problem. She tore up the paper toweling I kept spotless on the cage floor into little bitty bits and she packed it down. Wherever. I surrendered. I bought her white cotton string. I read that babies can get their feet tangled in string, so I cut off three inch pieces and meticulously separated them out into fine threads and placed them on a bar in the cage. She was delighted! Felicity did not lose a minute and she set to work demonstrating herself to be a master nest builder. In all truth, I never saw another canary in my subsequent years who had the skills she had. She wove the fine cotton together in such a way that she created firm soft perfectly round, perfectly symmetrical nests set down in the little straw basket I attached safely to the inside of the cage, halfway between top and bottom. She was happy, I was fascinated and the whole event was enormously endearing.

Fernando was most obliging, jumping on her back and holding himself upright flapping his wings like a hummingbird. And next thing we knew Felicity was sitting on five eggs. Fernando, as it happened, was a good mate and fed her as she sat on the nest. Too cute.

As fate would have it all five eggs hatched perfectly, which is actually an unusually large surviving clutch, particularly for a novice canary breeder. But Felicity and Fernando knew what to do. I just watched and assisted as I could. They trusted me and I trusted the process and I knew I was enormously blessed to be witnessing it.

Fernando brought food diligently to Felicity and she fed the babies. Teamwork. Not much later I no longer had two fullgrown canaries. I had seven. Hmmmm.....

Months led to years and at the high point I had twenty-three canaries. We had grown to four cages. I named each one. Gradually I began feeling really overwhelmed. I felt a deep attachment to "my babies" and feared I would not be able to place them with folks who would give them the kind of care I had. And that mattered to me. Felicity's grandchildren. I knew all about them. Who could build good nests, who could not. (I called the latter girls' nests PreFabs as they threw their nests together in a haphazard fashion.) Who got along. Who did not. I walked the forest and gathered special wild herbs for them. Miner's lettuce. Dandelion leaves. The tiny little "purses" from shepherd's purse. They loved them all. Meanwhile a growing part of me began feeling burdened by keeping the cages cleaned. A voice in me said, "If I never clean another seed cup it will be too soon."

By the time I let them go I had buried both my dear Felicity and her devoted lovely Fernando and a few sons and daughters as well. Finally and at last I called a young breeder to whom I had given a couple of English budgies (yes, there were more) and said, "Come and get the canaries." I knew they would transition to an outdoor aviary where they could truly fly. I took comfort in knowing they would be cared for by someone with a deep interest in breeding birds, who worked at a feed and pet store (as you only find in towns that were once truly agricultural settings) and that he was not only knowledgeable but had access to all the supplies he would need at a discount. My beloved canaries left to begin a different life, together, as a flock, with a new owner and a different destiny. I grieved, but, oh the relief. I had had little idea that a simple pair of canaries would yield so much to care for. And I learned much, garnered much that fed my heart and mind and soul. And in the end I also learned that one must carefully weigh and choose what one commits to that might get out of hand. Each must make his own decision. Each must make the call of what to begin and when, and what to end and when. But inherent in the lesson is the caution to truly resist the temptation to plant more than we can honestly care for.

STAND FIRMLY ROOTED
IN THE GROUND

One particular and potentially strange Christmas, my daughter invited me to go on a cruise with her and her husband and mother-in-law. The details included my actually sharing a small ship's cabin with her mother-in-law. Quickly ascertaining that our lifestyle differences would make this a potentially uncomfortable situation, I politely declined. What, then, would I do for the holiday?

Sometime during the previous year one of my authors had mailed me a purple t-shirt with the name of a Mexican spa written across the front. Attached was a note telling me I should really go there one day. Maybe now was the day? And thus began one of my stranger holiday adventures.

In spite of the very short leadtime, I managed to book myself into this wonderful Mexican spa. One flies into the largest town nearby and they come for you in a bus and you arrive as a group. Everyone arrives on the same day of the week and everyone stays one week.

To my surprise there was an orientation meeting at 4:00 o'clock the first afternoon, shortly after our arrival. Each guest was given a blank schedule for the week and it was the guest's task to decide which activities he or she would be participating in throughout the week's stay. To my amazement I discovered that nearly all of the folks at my dining table that evening had already filled in most of their week's activities on their schedules!

"What will *you* be doing?" they asked politely.

"Massage?" I mumbled. There was nothing filled in on my schedule whatsoever. "I came to rest."

"Rest?" they said, and rolled their eyes.

It slowly began to dawn on me that the large majority of the folks in attendance that week were from the East Coast, particularly from New York, primarily Jewish, and not really interested in celebrating Christmas. I began to realize they were probably escaping the Christmas brouhaha, and they had, indeed, come to fight the winter blahs and to get in shape! They were on a mission. They were committed!

This was going to be a strange Christmas. I had never before placed myself in a situation where I was marginalized socially at Christmastime.

Nevertheless, I had Christmas to celebrate. I decided to go into town.

This in itself is moderately regarded as *verboden* at this spa. People go there to divest themselves of winter poundage with an ultraclean diet and a visit to town (which was, in fact a humble border town) bore the possibility of "cheating". The savvy guests even had a term for it. It was apparently called "going over the wall".

Where was I?

I had lived in Mexico for two years. I spoke fluent Spanish. I had hitchhiked all over half the country alone in my twenties, my daughter was born in Mexico City, and I was going to town. I secured a local taxi in front of the spa and off the driver and I went, into town. On the way I spotted a small decrepit tree lot selling Christmas trees. It was the saddest version of a Christmas tree lot I had ever seen in my life. I asked the driver to stop. Surprised, he did. And he waited as I purchased a small sad tree, the best of the lot, which he cooperatively lugged into the trunk. Undaunted, we continued into town and he told me where I might purchase some decorations. Warming up to the adventure, and doggedly determined to quietly and unobtrusively honor my own traditions I entered a small shop where I purchased some small and enchanting Mexican straw ornaments bound with red and green yarn, and a few handpainted tin figures, with which I was already familiar. And then to my delight I found red chili pepper lights! Wonderful. Coupled with a small string of twinkly multicolored lights, I was set.

My taxi driver returned me to the spa bearing the fruits of my trip into town. I'm sure a few eyebrows raised, but, everyone was basically polite. I dragged my purchases up the long trail to my own lodge and spent the rest of the afternoon putting up the tree, placing it before the window, and then adding the decorations. I kept at it until dinnertime, when I went back down the hill.

As fate would have it, I discovered once night was upon us, that the tree stood in a window lighted almost perfectly central to the entire spa property, up on a hill, shining down on all below. So much for unobtrusive observation. I began to feel slightly uncomfortable. I took some comfort knowing the staff was Catholic and perhaps would find the tree a welcome sight shining down on us below. Still, I felt unusually vulnerable.

As Christmas rapidly approached I was surrounded by guests running to classes all day. To aerobics. To yoga. To pilates. Early morning hikes. I had settled into one yoga class, a facial, and a daily massage. I eventually worked up to one morning hike that led offsite to the gardens where all the organic vegetables we were served at our meals were grown, and a splendid breakfast awaited us. The main gardener in charge was enormously charming and the chef extremely hospitable.

My plans and traditions did not feel complete. What would I be doing Christmas Eve? I went to the office and inquired of the desk clerk about local churches, as uncommon and unlikely as it might seem to be leaving the posh grounds. Yes, there was a main church where there would be midnight mass on Christmas Eve. I was heartened and expressed my interest in attending. Being a service-oriented spa, they offered me a van and driver. (They were probably also worried about liability and bad publicity if something happened to me, I'm certain.) But I was delighted. I would have my Christmas celebration, quietly in town.

To my immense mortification that evening at dinner an announcement was made over an intercom to all the guests dining in the large splendid hall that *I* was organizing a trip to the local church on Christmas Eve and to please see me for further information. I am not a shy person by any means, but I wanted to crawl under the table. I simply was not used to being in the small minority! Plain and simple. I recognized this as an enormously valuable opportunity to stay true to myself and to stand with dignity and grace for and in my own traditions. I realized that probably many of the people with whom I actually shared that particular Christmas had been subjected to marginalities that would make my own experience seem like nothing at all. I stood in that energy, my consciousness expanding with compassion for myself and those around me.

But I was not done. We needed wine. Didn't we? I went to the spa chef and told him I had a marvelous recipe for mulled wine. Would he make it if I bought the wine? He would. When guests learned of this they could hardly believe their ears. This simply was not done here. It was *that* year. I brought the wine. He dolled it up. Many shared it and we had a fine time.

Christmas Eve arrived and I was relieved to see that I was not the only person going to town. About five or six others had come out of the cultural woodwork to accompany me. It was dark when we arrived and the small and humble church was filling up with locals. I took a pew behind an exquisite elderly woman wearing a black lace veil. She turned her head to acknowledge me so graciously that tears welled up quickly in my eyes. How I loved the Mexican people and their innate warmth and charity and non-judgmental welcoming. I was at home. Tears streamed down my cheeks as I took part respectfully in their service, while staying towards the back of the church. My eyes scanned the simple altar and I took heart as I recognized a humble painting of the Virgin of Guadalupe, of whom I am very fond. Her likeness always graces an area near my front door wherever I am living in the form of a handcarved wooden figure from the depths of Nayarit.

This, then, was my special Christmas, one that challenged my perceptions and expectations and all that I take for granted. It became the perfect opportunity to stand firm in the ground in which I am rooted, wherever I might be.

SHARE GENEROUSLY YOUR BOUNTY

When my beloved grandmother turned 94 it became obvious that she at last could no longer care fully for herself and I made the choice to step in. She had always been a very good mother to me and I was not totally satisfied with the choices which had been made on her behalf. I consulted with my family, it was agreed upon, and very shortly after I found myself driving the two hours north, packing up my grandmother and what few possessions she was allotted in a nursing home (the bulk of her possessions to be sent down to me later by truck) and rerouting her life into the beauty and heart of California's wine country. We were extremely fortunate to have found a warm, friendly and caring nursing home in a very charming and lively town centered around a lush park with ducks and ponds, patterned on the Spanish style *zocolo*. The nursing home was within walking distance of this delightful park. Over the next six years this home for the frail and elderly became not only my grandmother's home, but my second home, where I became part of a community for which I really came to care.

To get to the nursing home I had to pass along a narrow two-lane road that ran through a small green valley lined with wineries and farms and small shops. I took great pleasure in traversing this road several times each week. Indeed, it became one of my favorites. One particular weekend I noticed a small cart full of fresh flowers in large white buckets by the roadside and what appeared to be a small Hispanic man wearing a white shirt who was selling them. I began wondering where these flowers had come from, and then I began wondering what became of the flowers they were not able to sell on the weekend. I paid closer attention as I passed that area of the road on my journeys and was able to determine that there was, in fact, a wholesale nursery set back from the road. One weekend I stopped and asked the man how I might contact the owner. I jotted down the information, called, arranged an appointment and the next Monday I met with the woman who owned the nursery.

In all honesty, we were quite fascinated with each other from the start. There was an immediate connection. She was from Denmark and I am partly of Danish descent and the conversation flowed easily. I told her of my grandmother's living situation and my care of her and at last I politely told her I had found myself wondering what became of the flowers they were not able to sell by Monday mornings. I was heartened when she told me they were recycled. When I told her I was interested in picking some of them up and taking them to the nursing home, and would she consider that, she was delighted! And so was I! And so it was agreed.

The next Monday I drove my truck to a small white refrigerated building on her property where she had asked me to meet her head gardener, where I would be picking up the leftover flowers. I was expecting perhaps two or three buckets of sunflowers or maybe a few colorful bouquets. As I parked the car a friendly Mexican came out to greet me and pointed to about thirty large buckets of every conceivable color of rose you could imagine. Purple. Red. White. Pink. Yellow. Buckets and buckets of roses! "These??" I exclaimed. "Yes," he responded, with a warm smile. My mind tried to grasp what he was telling me. Thirty buckets of roses. Longstemmed, huge roses. Stunned, I pushed my body into action as my mind tried to catch up to our good fortune, and packed the truck to the absolute brim with roses, barely leaving room for my two Border Collies in the front seat. I didn't know if they would all fit. I managed, and I drove deliriously, headily down Hwy. 12 towards the nursing home, looking into the rear view mirror on occasion and seeing only my face framed by literally hundreds and hundreds of gorgeous fat roses, an almost surreal experience, my face beaming hugely in the mirror. The scent was overbearing.

I arrived and backed my car onto the sidewalk before the nursing home, as if for delivery, and ran in and excitedly invited the head nurses outside. "Look!" I opened the back of the truck. "Look!! " They looked, stunned. Smiles slowly stretched across their faces as they realized what a gift we had been given. We searched shelves and cupboards and rooms for empty vases. We turned the front counter into an assembly line filling vases with roses and distributing them throughout the various common rooms. People gathered around the front desk in various states of joy and disbelief. Every table in the dining room was burgeoning with fragrant roses. All around the front desk, all the tables in the entryway, the crafts rooms. My grandmother's table next to her bed overflowed with radiant full deep red and white roses. What a joy! What a blessing!

The project became affectionately known as *Cada Lunes*. For the rest of that season, each Monday morning I arrived early at the nursery, packed up my truck with the roses and other flowers this benevolent wholesaler so generously offered us, and drove the flowers to the place that served as a safe and caring haven for my beloved grandmother and dozens of other men and women. These flowers brightened their days enormously. Many of these women had been gardeners themselves, had lovingly tended their own rose gardens. The sheer joy of arriving at their meals and finding the entire room filled to the brim with beautiful flowers was an unexpected, immeasurable delight and it filled my heart knowing that through the grace of inspiration and generosity this was made possible. A simple question. A simple answer. What opportunities lie within our reach that hold the power to make a difference in the quality of the lives of others simply by sharing the bounties and blessings that grace our lives?

BUILD SOUND FENCES

Nearly all of my adult life my cats were allowed to go outside as they pleased. One of these cats was a big fluff of a champagne-orange tabby with pale green eyes named Honeypot, who had been given to me by my friend Patty. She had gallantly rescued him and two of his feral littermates. Oh, he was a wild and spitting thing, not to be touched. I had to bring him home in a big box, which I placed in my bedroom and closed the door. And there I left him in that dark and quiet box, to settle down, for hours. Meanwhile I made a soft place for him in the back of the closet and put out food and water. And at the end of the day I carefully turned over the box and out he tipped and ran for cover in the closet, as I expected. And there I left him, asleep, not on the soft blanket in the corner, but atop a shoe. Sometime in the middle of the night I got up and gently picked him up and I brought him to bed with me, and put him on my neck and there he slept, purring. While it's true he saw nothing beyond those four walls for his first week, truly, he crossed over very quickly. We came to know him as the most gentle and affectionate of souls, and we loved him dearly.

One of my very favorite memories of Honeypot happened on the day we left Mendocino for good. The truck was loaded, we were set to leave and I could not find my Honeypot. I wandered up the narrow road through the forest, calling and calling him. "Honeypot! Honeypot! Here, kitty kitty kitty kitty!" Finally I heard him calling back to me, and I looked and there he was, a soft orange beauty standing in the palest of sunlight that fell gently on the forest floor. The poignancy of this moment was not lost on me. This was the last image of the end of our Mendocino adventure. The last page. We were ending this chapter together, and beginning another. I took in this precious moment and then called, "Come here, Honeypot! It's time to leave. Come on, kitty. Come on, my boy." And he ran into my arms and that was the last thing to do. We got into the truck and drove away.

So Honeypot had always lived outside, always known the deeper forests, much deeper than I or the dogs. But he always came back safe and sound and he was happy. In the evenings when he returned from his wanderings, he would jump into a comfy lap and nudge one's neck. Everyone who knew him and loved him (and there were many) knew that about him.

When our Luna cat came to live with us in Santa Rosa, Honeypot more or less accepted her. Occasionally they even did things together. One morning I came out onto the deck and looked down into the garden and each of them was standing atop six foot tall stakes that held the fence around the garden and each from his vantage point was surveying the land. I could barely believe my eyes and I ran for my camera. This photo became a cherished possession.

One evening I could not find Luna. I called and called but she did not come in. I went to bed, very worried. My cats always slept in the house at night. They never stayed out. Too many critters.

The next morning I went out to call her again, and as I came close to the garage, which was further up the hill, I heard a mew, and heartened, threw open the garage door and out she walked. I was thrilled! I had been convinced she had been eaten up by the woods as woods are sometimes wont to do. And you never really know what happened.

I picked her up in my arms and carried her back into the house, telling her how happy I was to have found her. And I showed her to Honeypot.

"Look, Honeypot! Look! I found Luna!"

Honeypot was not amused. He seemed agitated. He went to the front door and asked to go out. I opened the door per his request. Just prior to leaving, he straightened his shoulders back, and lifted his head, as if in some kind of resolve, and out he leaped in one big bound. And he was gone. I closed the door.

That afternoon I heard Peaches and Moxie barking their heads off out on the deck. They were both fenced in, so could not take off. I left my desk and went to see what they were fussing about. Peaches looked back at me two or three times, kind of pleading, I realized in retrospect, but I looked around and could not see a thing, so I surmised they had seen a flock of crows in a nearby tree, which they loved to bark at. "I don't see anything," I told them, and I went back inside to my work.

Moments later I saw a strange dog in my front garden. I had not seen this dog since it was a puppy, but I knew who it was. It was half pit bull, half lab. I had had misgivings hearing this dog was coming to live on our hill, but my questions were rebuffed. The mottled dog was scratching up the turf of the grass, the way dogs do when they are finished with something they have been doing. I was slightly alarmed, as it was very unusual for a strange dog to show up on my remote property, but I said at the time, "No wonder they were barking." And left it at that. I watched the dog head off the property, glad it had left.

That night I could not find Honeypot, which was highly unusual. Two cats in two nights? I went to bed and I had a dream. In the dream I saw Honeypot sitting on a stump in the woods. I recognized the location on my property. Honeypot's fur in the dream was slightly transformed. He looked like his fur was almost ablaze with a reddish glow. I looked in the direction he was looking in the dream. He was watching two animals playing in the grass, off behind the old barn. One of the animals was spotted. There was something unusual about the playing. I woke up and reviewed the dream and I said to myself, "That cat is dead."

When it got light, I went outside and looked near where Honeypot had shown me the two animals had been playing and under one edge of the barn I found his beautiful dead body, matted about the throat with grasses.

Shocked, I picked him up and carried him to the deck where I wept over him as I cleaned his body, all the while trying to understand. Later I dug a deep hole and buried him just outside the back corner of my fenced garden, just under the very stake he had climbed with Luna, placing a large heavy rock on his grave. I printed out a copy of a poem I loved, and placed it on the grave, holding it in place with a jar full of flowers. Later I purchased and planted a blue clematis on the fence next to the grave, honoring him in every way I could think to.

It was not until the next day that I connected all the dots and realized that the pit bull mix had entered my property and had killed my dear Honeypot and that Honeypot had shown me exactly what had happened and where to look. I must have been too in shock to put it all together as it happened.

Fear struck my heart. I knew there was no guarantee that this would never happen again. The owners were contacted. They were defensive, not sympathetic and it was clear they were afraid of any legal responsibility. It was ironic that I discovered at that point in my process that if the dog came back to do harm, if he attacked my rooster, my Chanticleer, that as long as I posted a warning sign that said something about "worrying the livestock" I could legally shoot the dog. But if he attacked my cat or dogs, I could do nothing. That was the law. Chickens were protected. They were "livestock". Pets were not. I was shocked.

I decided to build a fence.

I called my Mexican gardeners. They told me what I had to buy. I went to the hardware store and bought everything you need to fence in four acres of land on two sides. (Fortunately the back side and one side were already fenced, though this did no good considering the direction this dog lived.) Then I bought a long green cattle gate and heavy posts on which to hang it and cement to put in the posts. I made certain that the wiring on the cattlegate would not allow for any dog to come through on to my property.

We began the work. This was major work, in the woods. We got permission to use t-stakes that already ran along my neighbor's property, strung with barbed wire, making the third side easier. He was delighted. He promptly went out and bought two cows who were then securely housed on his property. These were the cows who wore cowbells that we heard ever after but rarely saw.

I learned about fenceposting. I bought the tool. My Mexican gardeners laughed and sang as they moved through the woods posting the stakes for the fence, and then mounting the wire. Another day they came and brought their entire families. I bought them all pizza and we had a pizza party in the woods with the wives and the children. I brought them water to refresh themselves as they sang their songs in Spanish, making their way through the woods, making it safe for me and my animals. Making sure what happened to my beloved Honeypot could never happen again.

It was a good fence. Things lined up. There were four apple trees in the orchard that ended up on the "wrong side of the fence". I lent them to my neighbor. I told him, "As long as I am here, these are now your apple trees. You tend them as you please, and you reap the apples." He was quite pleased with that arrangement.

There is something very specifically healthy about strong fences and boundaries. They first of all are a way of taking intrinsic care of yourself and those you love. But energetically something else happens as well. Things fall into place.

What are the sound fences you have built to take care of yourself and those you love?

FEEL NOT OBLIGED TO MAKE GOOD USE OF EVERY RIPE FRUIT ON THE VINE

While living in Sonoma County on these four acres of land at the end of a dirt road there happened to be, as mentioned, a lovely apple orchard at the entrance to the property. This gave me the opportunity to learn about tending to twenty-three trees. During my first winter there, there was an early freeze and subsequently not that many apples emerged in the springtime. Imagine my surprise when in the second spring each tree's limbs hung towards the ground under the weight of hundreds of apples. A full crop. What to do? In the beginning I diligently and happily climbed a ladder and picked blemish-free apples and mailed a large box to my parents and a large box to my daughter, being careful to have them approved by the local agricultural office before putting them in the mail so as not to unwittingly introduce some hidden menacing bug into another territory. They were always pronounced as fine. Then there was the round of picking for my own self. My canaries loved the abundant fresh organic fruit. Next an offer to neighbors, many of whom had their own trees to harvest. I felt the urgency to share the abundance and my good fortune. I began feeding apples from the ground to the donkey and horse next door, whose fences ran across the edge of my property. They joyfully complied and I discovered that they began to do all their daylong grazing along my fenceline in hopes that I might emerge and toss them some fallen apples. Their owners hardly saw them! The apples continued to ripen and fall. What to do? I decided to call every food relief society within a two-county range to see if I could get someone to come pick the apples for hungry families. Sadly, I could not find a single agency who felt they had the manpower and/or insurance coverage to come pick apples for needy families.

I heard from one of the agricultural experts that coddling moths would be making their homes happily within any apples on the ground. One morning I gathered an entire orchard's worth of fallen apples from the ground and put them in the recycling bin. Gone. Apples continued to fall. The horse and donkey and canaries burst with apples. I bought a dehydrator. I dried apples for Christmas presents, after dipping them in lemon water and cinnamon and sugar. Yummy, but very time consuming. What does one do with so many apples? Where does it end? I had apples in boxes on the back deck. I had apples in the refrigerator. I had apples in bowls in the kitchen. I took apples to my grandmother's nursing home. Must I do something with all of them?

Very unexpectedly a new critter appeared on our hill. A lovely blonde mama coyote with her baby. She loved the apples. She was hungry and had a new baby to feed. By this time the end of the season was nearing and apples stubbornly clung to branches, withering. I begin to shake the trees allowing the last apples of the season to fall. I left them for mama coyote. I advised both Cheyenne the donkey and Reno the horse that all subsequent apples would fall to the mama and her babe. But Cheyenne protested vociferously. She bucked. She brayed. She tossed her head and loudly hee-hawed as each morning I would walk to the orchard with my dogs and not feed her. Most mornings we would see mama coyote scamper out of the orchard into the surrounding pine forest.

So the season ends. And I realize that I am not obliged to make good use of every ripe fruit on the vine. The Earth and its inhabitants will naturally recycle what I am not able to use. It will be someone else's joy and benefit. I can count on a master plan. I realize that life offers us myriad choices and that as we say yes to some, and no to others we might feel we have missed out on something, or that others, like Cheyenne, might protest loudly at our choices, feeling abandoned and not understanding. Choices we must make, however, and trust that whatever is left behind will serve a fellow being,

MISTAKE NOT ONE PLANT
FOR ANOTHER

I first learned about paper wasps from one of The Bug Guys, which is what I affectionately called the entomologists who worked at the local mosquito abatement office in Sonoma County. Ed. He knew so much about bugs! It was his job to rid the North Bay of destructive critters. "Vector control," he called it. You could call those guys about mosquitoes, but you could also call them about, say, yellow jackets. Yellow jackets in California are known for their aggressive ways. They will attack you totally unprovoked, especially if you have meat anywhere in the vicinity. This includes pet food. I had relied on Ed to come more than once after finding yellow jacket nests in the ground on my property up in the woods, close to my house. He would pull up in his county truck, step out and slowly don a big white suit and netted mask, and within minutes

117

he'd have extracted the scary nest and have them out of there. Once he showed me a nest he had dug up on someone's property. I could not believe how big it was! It looked like a huge roll of some strange organic paper, layers and layers, rolled into a continuous nest, with a large community of yellow jackets layered within it. Quite a system. And a pity to destroy, but better that than a dog or cat or other animal stumbling into it and taking a beating. Oldtimers in the county poured kerosene down the holes of the yellow jackets' nests at night, after the yellow jackets had retired, and lit a match. I preferred Ed's way.

I'd had other adventures with the bug guys. They first came to help me in Marin County with a modest mosquito problem I had in my garden, and I was frankly amazed when they took the time to teach me about that species of mosquito. Maybe it's because I asked so many questions. But who else would teach you how to sex a treehole mosquito? They taught me! (He's the one with the fuzzy little doodang.) I got such a kick out of this, I became a real fan. That was also the trip when I pointed out a scorpion to them in my garage and they were just beside themselves, thrilled. They picked him up gently and took him back to their office in a jar. Yessir. Another breed, entomologists!

Another time I had these strange little bitty flies in my house, for some strange reason gravitating to the tv at night. I knew my *compadres* would know the answer. I caught a few and taped them to a file card and mailed the card up to their office. You can imagine my delight when I received a note back from one of them saying, "Thank you for the sewer fly bookmark!"

Funny guys.

They also taught me about carpenter bees, which I had never seen before. If you haven't, they are very large dark bees that nose around your wood looking for a place to, essentially, drill a nest. I can understand why homeowners wouldn't be fond of them, but I feel especially protective and am very fond of them. I am charmed by their focus and size and intent. I think they have an excellent work ethic, and I think of them as the teddybears of the bee clan.

The absolutely worst thing they taught me about was the day I called them and told them there were "all these flies in my house!" Green flies. Dozens of them. Really. Against the window. I was killing them as fast as I could. What were they? "Is there any chance something died under your house?" Oh, I hope not. An investigation into a closet disclosed a very unpleasant odor from somewhere under the floorboards. Oh, dear. They were very reassuringly philosophical. Apparently (as if you need to know this) there is a flesh-eating fly that will come and rid you of what has crawled under your house as its final resting place. These are the things you learn living in the country in the woods. "They'll be gone in about four days, Kathryn." And they were.

It was natural, then, that I would turn again to these wonderful men when I found something I thought was a form of yellow jacket (boo hiss) forming a nest on the roof over my back deck. I noticed they were skinnier, but they were the same familiar black with yellow stripes. Alarmed, I called Ed immediately, and within an hour or two I heard the opening and closing of my cattlegate down by the orchard, alerting me someone was entering the property. Up drove Ed in his official white truck and he stepped out, ready to take them away. My hero. I took him around back to show him where they were setting up their new home.

You can imagine my surprise when a half smile crossed his face as he looked up in the corner and said, "You know these wasps won't really hurt you and you don't really have to take them down." What? They are wasps! "Yes, it's true they are wasps," he said, " but they are paper wasps. They are actually very gentle and easy to live around. They are not aggressive. I don't think you will find them to be a problem." I could scarcely believe my ears. Unconvinced, I listened on.

"Kathryn, there are probably only a few dozen wasps in that entire nest. There's just one queen doing all this building. Paper wasps don't build big colonies. If you watch them fly, they are kind of slow. And if you don't bother them, they won't bother you."

I was slowly warming up to the idea. This was Ed, my bug guy. He must know. Right?

It was clear from his body language, hands stuffed in his pockets and keeping his respectful distance from the nest, that he did not want to destroy the nest and saw no need for it. This was a stretch for my belief systems, but I decided I could give it a rather reluctant try. I was still having a very hard time believing I could coexist peacefully with a nest of wasps very close to my back door, just above my head on a deck that was used a good portion of the summer by myself, my animals and friends.

And so he left. And I was there with the paper wasps. Country experiment number 223.

Over the next few days merging into weeks I kept a close eye on the paper wasps. What I found to my surprise and delight, was that Ed really knows his stuff. They are good neighbors. That summer I learned (and, oh, I'm glad!) that paper wasps are actually very peace-loving creatures. They do not buzz about your head or body. They stay with their own kind. They might swoop slowly down and check something out, but for the most part, they are busy building and tending their small unobtrusive nests, doing what they need to do to live and survive and they have no interest in humans or animals or other creatures. They are just doing their thing. And it's a lovely thing. They fly with a slow and gentle grace that is endearing. I learned to not only accept them but welcome them year to year. I enjoyed their rhythms and the very slow enchanting patterns of their flight as they came and went during the day. They are quite lovely. And never ever did they once trespass into the house or upon anyone else who shared their space.

When confronted with a new critter what lenses do we look through? Do we take the time to inform ourselves to find out if this is truly what we think it is? Do we consider for a minute the creature might be a source of delight and a valued member of our family of life? Or do we make assumptions? Who are the paper wasps in your life? An unexpected source of joy and pleasure and a kindred soul?

APPRECIATE SMALL RETURNS

She was sitting calmly in the middle of the drive just beyond our house and I impulsively did what I *always* did when any strange cat arrived on our four acre wooded property. I told my Border Collie, Moxie, to chase her off. I did this knowing that Moxie would never hurt a strange cat, but was very skilled at chasing animals that did not "belong" to the edge of the woods and then she would return. Moxie moved toward the cat, but instead of heading back into the woods the cat ran immediately to the stairs of the deck and curled up on her back, feet extended. This stopped Moxie flat and I was immediately alarmed. This was not normal cat behavior and there was something wrong with this cat. I protectively called Moxie to me and watched this slinky Siamese skirt off into the grasses of the side yard, flicking her head from side to side, and slithering like a snake through the grass. My immediate thought was rabies. I put my animals safely back into the house and watched from safe advantage from my deck. She (he?) was hiding in the bushes. I knew it.

My mother instinct kicked in (wouldn't you know?) and I placed a dish of cat food out in the garden, but the cat did not emerge. This only added to my alarm. An hour later I saw her again, hiding under a yellow margarita bush. How curious. Where did she come from? What did she want? Was she sick? Hungry? Obviously she was afraid.

Over the next six weeks an amazing and painstaking journey began to unfold, as days later I discovered that this small feral cat, clearly not full-grown, had taken up a safe post under the small cabin that served as guesthouse, in the front garden. She had my full attention and my fears were replaced by a deepening concern.

I researched Siamese cats on the Net. I found a Siamese cat breeder who wrote, "It is clearly recorded that in 1884 the departing British Consul-General Gould was given a Siamese cat by the Siamese king as a farewell gift, and considered it as a great honor since the cat came from those bred in the palace by the royal family." Photos of traditional "applefaced" Siamese cats on her site looked remarkably like our visitor, and strengthened my resolve to tame her.

Pondering the Siamese's historical story I found myself thinking again and again, "This is not what the King of Siam had in mind," and I grieved that his gift had run so far astray from the original intent, for here was the clear offspring of that gift, wild, lost and abandoned deep in the woods of Northern California. What had transpired between these two events? Many things, not all conscious or loving or fitting that original impulse. This pulled at my heartstrings and I wanted to make things more right.

I created a place for her on the porch of this cabin, and offered food, water and a small soft rug showing good intent and generosity of spirit, which clearly any wounded creature would recognize. Right?

Eventually, usually at dusk, she would slither out, again snapping her head from right to left. She would then furtively eat, once she reassured herself that we were safely back inside our house. We watched intently from the front picture window, I with my binoculars, and Peaches, my second Border Collie, relying on her keen eyesight. I tried to show Luna, my Maine Coon, but she would have none of it. Over time our little orphan slowly gained confidence and trust, so that each evening she would allow herself to increasingly linger a few minutes after her meal. We celebrated by naming her Sweet Pea.

Gradually, I introduced a little game to her, a healing journey, indeed, that entailed putting her food out on her porch each morning, then retreating back to the house, my starting point. She would suspiciously emerge, but hunger would win out and she would begin to eat. Each time she turned her back I would take one step forward. She would whirl around and I would be standing still as a mouse. Then when she resumed eating I would take another step forward. (I always felt like I was playing Mother May I!) Part of the game was for her to never actually see me moving. I would simply be closer. I remained, however, exceedingly still. It was fun. Each day I would play this game, always with the intent of encouraging her to let me a bit closer each day. Sometimes this worked and other times she would not stand for a single step forward and would run very close to the ground and out of sight under the cabin, lickety split. It was slow but steady progress.

One morning while weeding, I unexpectedly found her curled up fast asleep in a protected sunny patch up the hill from the cabin. Quietly I said, "Kitty." Then, "Kitty?" Then "Kitty???" until I realized with sorrow that she was completely deaf. Clapping my hands verified this. She remained fast asleep as she couldn't hear a thing! It then dawned on me why she'd been whipping her head about: it was the only way she could "see" if she was safe 360 degrees around her. Her ears were of no use to her survival in the woods. The impact of realizing this deaf Siamese cat had survived who knows how long all the treacheries in our woods overwhelmed me. What a brave creature and what a respite she had found, and no wonder the underside of that cabin must be looking so very good to her. And food. My.

To my utter dismay, one day Sweet Pea did not come around. I looked high and low but my search revealed no kitty. I did what I could to extend my search further uphill, but being in the middle of a forest, this was a tough task. I alerted neighbors, though no one ever saw her.

Then miraculously and inexplicably a few days later she blessedly "came home". I literally wept for joy, and her return only strengthened my resolve to try to bring her into the safety and comfort of our clan. We picked up our long, slow journey of establishing trust.

It was fully five weeks into the process when Sweet Pea would allow me to get as close as six feet away *if* I made only minimal movements and sat on the ground to appear much smaller and less threatening. She also had begun a pattern of coming out from under the cabin and sitting under a large pink oleander bush, safely out of reach, where she would sit and howl. Very endearing. However any attempt to approach her sent her scurrying to the safety of the dark spidery confines under the cabin.

I decided we needed something "safe" to bridge us. I found a stick. I tied one of Luna's toys, sporting lots of pink feathers, to the end of the stick and introduced it to Sweet Pea while she was safely under the cabin. Picture me lying on the ground poking this long stick with feathers on it under the cabin towards a cat I could not really see. It worked. Sort of. At least I had a cat striking viciously at the feathers. It was unnerving, I admit. It was not exactly kitten play. It was more like playing "kill". But it was a start. I tried my best to keep my fingers safely at *my* end of the stick . It was an awkward but successful dance. Fear at both ends of the stick.

We continued this daily. I introduced a blanket to lie on as we played our feather game. Then one sweet day something different happened, and together we entered the blessed world of transformation. Instead of batting at the toy with those dangerous outstretched claws, Sweet Pea rubbed up against the stick! I was thrilled and dumbfounded! I recognized before me a creature wanting to be touched. So touch I did, very gingerly, very, very cautiously, as I was as afraid as she. But I touched her and she responded with a very clear message she liked that very much, thank you and would like more. Yes, indeed. And more she got. By the very next day I was miraculously putting both hands under her tummy and lifting her gently away from the ground, allowing her feet to stay touching the Earth, however. Within days I could lift her fully off the ground.

Once this crossing over happened, the process accelerated. I lured her into the guesthouse to sleep at night. I taught her about litter boxes, a haphazard affair at best. We experimented with toys. The dance slowly shifted from one of wild predator not quite to be trusted, to a cat sincerely getting the hang of the concept of play! Each day small victories were won. She went willingly into a kennel. She went to the vet, where Doctor Nick complained with a big smile that he could not hear her heartbeat because she was purring too loudly! Sweet Pea inched toward socialization, cooperation, training, and being with us.

Shortly after, I put Sweet Pea in a small blue kennel just above a second kennel containing Luna, whom she still did not know, and drove her across country to her new home in North Carolina. She ate her meals on cue balanced on the back of the bumper while on a lead, from California to Appalachia, like a gypsy trouper.

Today Sweet Pea is a full member of the family. Luna is her very best friend and they do almost everything together. All winter they wrap and cuddle themselves into furry kaleidoscopic poses to keep warm. Each morning they perch on a stool next to the screen door and they peer out into the garden together. They climb the bookcase and sleep on top. They stand together at the glass front door noting the parade of birds and chipmunks and squirrels that enter and leave our garden stage each morning.

Joyfully, step by step, Sweet Pea opened to a new life, crossing fully into love and security, never a part of her life until she stepped into ours.

May your lives be so blessed.

LET YOUR GROUND LIE FALLOW

I have to confess that I am busy mostly from early morning until night. (Then I get eight hours of sleep, the cornerstone of my good health.) But I make lists. I do. I have a very active List Maker who lives inside me. And I usually get it all done. And then I make more lists.

As I told a friend recently, I sometimes have to trick myself into doing nothing. Here is the trick I sometimes play on myself.

I learned that in the Native American tradition there are practices built on the Four Directions. Each of the directions represents an area of one's life. And as this is a wholistic model, if you practice and honor each of the Four Directions you will be covered, so to speak. And I learned, happily, that the direction North is the direction of doing nothing. So if my List Maker gets antsy because I'm not "doing something" because I'm not, I tell my List Maker, in my internal dialogue with her, "I'm doing something. I'm doing North." And what can she say to that? Really?

I do take Power Naps. I find I sometimes do need them and they give me exactly what I need on those days that by early afternoon my energy is waning. I've found that between 1:00-2:00 PM is a good time for me to do this. It doesn't work for me to begin after 2:30 PM at the latest, as I would then have trouble getting to sleep at night. I know each person's body and rhythm is different. But here is what I do.

First, I lie perpendicular to how I normally sleep. This gives my body and mind the message instantly that I am not lying down to "go to bed"; I am lying down for a particular purpose, and it's to just restart my engine, and it will be short.

Secondly I lie flat on my back. Then I put an eye pillow over my eyes. (In the South they call them eye bags.) Most eye pillows are made of silk. They are about four inches by eight inches in size. They have flax seeds inside which have an interesting feel from the outside. Kind of smooth and gentle and flowing. Nothing bulky. And most importantly they contain herbs that promote relaxation like chamomile and lavender flowers and sometimes lemongrass. The scents are natural and subtle and our bodies seem to automatically respond to them in an instinctively relaxing way.

My using an eye pillow serves several purposes. First, it adds to the inner programming that I am simply taking a Power Nap and that this will be short. Secondly, it feels good. Then I have the advantage of the herbs helping me relax. And I'm blocking out the light, which will stimulate melatonin production in my body and allow me to sleep briefly midday.

I personally put my arms at my sides. If I curl up in a fetal position or any position that is reminiscent of what I do at night, I will not be in keeping with the programming I need at that moment.

And then I go to sleep. I will invariably wake up in about fifteen minutes. I feel rested, never groggy and I acquire whatever boost I needed to keep me going until evening.

Letting your ground lie fallow has varying implications, of course. It could be as simple as a Power Nap or could mean taking a vacation is in order, or it could mean that you need a long dry spell between relationships or jobs in order to rekindle whatever it is you need to access to assist you in living the life you were meant to live in the best possible light and way. Somehow our culture does not support the notion of taking a break. Europeans wisely take long holidays each summer and those days are built into the culture. Being as driven as we are, for whatever reasons, we don't do that.

What is it you need to do to integrate the notion of allowing the ground of your being to sometimes lie fallow?

DEEPLY TILL THE
HARDENED GROUND

It was my father's sister, Annie, who really introduced me to genealogy. She tended that fire slowly, only periodically mailing me this file or that, which I would glance over in a kind of foggy blur of moderate interest, and file away for One Day. I don't remember when One Day arrived and I really got hooked, but I did. Perhaps it was when I got intrigued in the mystery surrounding a particular aunt in the 1700's where family stories collided mightily with historical records. That was probably my entry point into my own long-term family history and I've been digging ever since.

My family of origin was rather insular and thus I did not grow up actually knowing how deep my American roots are, particularly on my father's side, which date back to Massachusetts in the early 1600's. Regardless, in genealogy circles my Halls are referred to as the Halls of Bristol County (Massachusetts) and people who have done a lot of research on the various Hall families would most likely recognize and could pinpoint my family by a single marriage, which, until recently, thanks to the miracles of DNA testing, had been locked in generations of dispute, known to researchers as "a brick wall", the plague—and sticky glue—of anyone doing genealogy. So the Halls and their descendants gather around the cyberspace fire to debate. And explore. And speculate. And argue. And to solve. And those before us did it without the benefit of computers and DNA research. And we know about them. And praise them. And read their notes and books. And ponder. And try our best to reconcile and repair and expand.

What is the real value of genealogy, you might wonder? I have friends who ask me that question, who find that being consumed by this life is quite enough without rummaging around in the past over a bunch of land deeds, birth and marriage certificates, church records and the treasures of various historical societies, looking for clues. I think of the entire process, first and foremost, as the Ultimate Jigsaw Puzzle—my own. Highly personalized. I am gradually getting a vivid sense of the adventurous men and women who came before me to America, their places of origin, their place in history—and thus my own. It is because of them, and their choices, ultimately, that I am here. And I think about them and thank them for their courage and sacrifices. I am also fascinated by their lives and the fact that I am able to access their histories, patchworking a larger puzzle where my own face emerges.

Several years ago I researched and wrote a history of my maternal grandmother. I recognize my immediate family contribution and I'm also aware that someone I will likely never meet will treasure it, someone whose history here has yet to begin. The front page of the history bears a reproduction of a large and lovely embroidery of red and blue flowers she completed in her twenties that today hangs framed in my kitchen against a blue wall. This cover was a way of continuing to honor her memory and her creativity that she offered so generously to our family over many many decades. She lived to be 100 years old, then gracefully slipped towards heaven. "Will my mother remember me?" she asked me in her final days. "It's been so long." I lovingly assured her she was waiting on the other side and would welcome her as her beloved daughter. And thus the family ties continue.

One of the most fun aspects of doing genealogy is meeting distant cousins! For increasing numbers of folks the notion of finding someone in cyberspace who shares a greatgreatgreatgreat uncle is a delight to the mind and heart! I met such a cousin a few years ago who owns a very old cherry dresser that belonged to our Connecticut Halls! This is the stuff that puts meat on the bones of our departed relatives, to have in our presence something which belonged to someone we have been researching for years. To find a photo of the very ship that carried a greatgreataunt across the Atlantic to America's teeming shores. To find a name on a monument, on a grave, barely legible in a Bible. The photo of a large home used as a field hospital during the Civil War, knowing your family member died there. Each little discovery from the past is such a precious gem in the family story. One name at a time. One grave at a time. One faded will at a time. One family at a time. Always filling in the story until one's place in it begins to clearly appear and a sense of connection and rootedness and, yes, common sense comes to the fore.

There is also a mystery to genealogy. It's a realm where one cannot, dare not, draw any conclusions, but to learn that the Connecticut Hall homesteads were only miles from where I went to high school in Massachusetts is utterly fascinating to me. The Midwest college I went to (I learned years later) was in the same county as a large parcel of land that was owned by my pioneering ancestors, only a short distance from where I studied. A greatgreatgreatgreat uncle who had come west for the Gold Rush, was revealed to be one of the early pioneers in Marin County, my home for over thirty years; thus I traversed the very same roads as he, lived in the very same valley. These discoveries are not just factual; they are visceral.

During the nineties it was in vogue in certain men's movement workshops to ask the entire group to stand. They stood.

"Name your father," the workshop leader would tell them.

They would all name their fathers.

"Name your grandfather."

Most would name their grandfathers.

"Name your greatgrandfather."

Fewer voices would respond.

"Name your greatgreatgrandfather."

Perhaps one man or two could name his father's greatgrandfather. Commonly the room by now would be silent.

Our lives and the lives of our children are dominated by the voice of the media against which we compare ourselves and find our sense of place on a daily basis. How thorough a mirror and context is what we find in our immediate reality? How is it that we have lost sight of our own true roots? And what might it mean to reclaim them?

PRUNE RIGOROUSLY WITH FAITH
THAT NEW LIFE WILL RETURN

Unless she was raised at her mother's knee, any experienced gardener will likely tell you that she was very tentative at first about pruning. For the uninitiated the act of taking sheers to branch and limb and stem is daunting, and understandably so. What if I cut back too much? Do it wrong? It dies? But pruning is not just about entering new territory. It's also about holding on. About fear and attachments. We hold on to plants that are clearly beyond rescuing, clothes we will never wear, jobs that drain us silly, friendships we have outgrown, machines that are obsolete and books we will never read.

Get the sheers!

Most of us by now have at least heard the term "feng shui", which is essentially a practice of the simplification and the harmonization of one's life, taking many factors into consideration. You don't just toss out a bunch of stuff, hang up some mirrors and windchimes, drop in a plant here or there and it's done. Instead, the practice of feng shui begins with a rigorous, thorough and very honest examination that begins on the outside, our physical surroundings, the things we choose to call ours, the spaces in which we live, and moves slowly into the inner realms, all the while honing in on refining both our inner and outer realities, until where we live and who and what we live with is a match. Our outer lives harmonize with the deepest essence of who we truly are.

I began with my clothes. That's an easy place to start. First round for me was simply letting go of everything I didn't really like or wear anymore. My friend Brenda told me to add another question, which was very valuable to my elimination process. She said to ask, "Would I buy it in a store today?" As I held aloft or tried on each article of clothing I own, asking myself this question gave me a new measuring stick of making sure my wardrobe reflected who I am *now*. And still the process can be rather overwhelming. So what do you do?

Simple answer. Make three piles. Keep. Sell. Give away. Better to keep eight outfits you love than twenty you hate. Also better five of quality than ten so-so's you bought-because-they-were-such-a-good-deal. There is no good deal to having poor quality greeting you in the morning. Then go through the Keep Pile again and sort out all the Mends. And then have them mended.

I personally go a couple of steps further. I have all my clothes arranged first by what they are: skirts, pants, tops, etc. And then I arrange by color. It saves me so much time. And the colors move through the spectrum. Black to brown to green to blue to purple to red to pink to orange to golds to beige to white. Dressy clothes and coats have their own closets.

Once you have gradually put yourself through this process, you will be delighted at the results. Imagine a closet that brings you joy when you open the door! You will begin the day with colorful, fun choices, with clothes that truly reflect your best you. This is a basic form of self-love, and this simple mirror, your new closet, will reflect back this message to your inner you.

Now, while we are in the bedroom, the primary room where you restore yourself so you can live your life, here are some bottom lines. Nothing superfluous. No piles! Clean, streamlined, pretty. Drawers in order. I once threw out 32 pairs of socks I had collected over the years. I took them to a place that works with the homeless who put them to very good use, which made me feel very good.

Books and magazines. As a book publicist and writer you can imagine I have tons of books. I did. I sorted through them and took bags of books down to the local used bookstore. To maintain, I frequently donate books to my local library—a win for the community and a win for me. Magazines can be readily taken to nursing homes, doctors' offices, or shelters. Pick a recipient that makes you feel good.

In your kitchen very simple rules can apply: only pragmatic *and* aesthetic things stay. A place for everything and everything in its place. Organization is critical to a well running kitchen. Also it's good to assess if anything is missing and purchase that when you are able. It is not "feng shui" to be using a hammer to open nuts; buy the nutcracker. Or using the sieve to sift flour; buy the flour sifter. Buy the nutmeg grater and the pastry blender. These small additions will lend a flow and appropriateness to your work. And flow is what you are looking for.

One important principle in feng shui is that *everything* must be repaired. A few years ago I had all of my grandmother's lamps, which I inherited, rebuilt. They now all sport the proper finials on top and they all have the appropriate new shades. These simple repairs have resulted in a very positive energy shift in my home, not just with the addition of the light itself, but in the honoring of my grandmother's precious gifts to me, and thus the family heritage. In this same vein I also had her wedding rings cleaned and all the diamonds checked and reset. Then I had them resized, truly an honoring—they can now be worn (and used). This breathes new life and opportunity into these precious rings. This is very much in keeping with my understanding and appreciation of feng shui.

Here is another tip. Be aware of anything and everything you have in your environment that has any negative association for you, that the second you see it you can feel some little emotional letdown. (Note: I'm not talking about nostalgia.) It doesn't matter why. Maybe you need to do a little accompanying ritual of forgiveness or grief work or anger release. But let the darn thing go, even if it's wonderful. It's bringing you down. Give it to someone who will not have that association, who can appreciate it. Let go, let go, let go. This is your new mantra. Your home and office are the stages for the unfolding drama of your life. Upgrade the energy. This is another form of sensitive self-love.

One area where there is the most danger of being out of keeping with basic feng shui principles are those areas we think of as places to store things, like the garage, the shed and the basement. These are infamous catch-all places, where things you will never, ever use are collecting dead energy thus keeping the energy in your home stuck. This is probably the least fun project and the hardest to get to. And, honestly? I've discovered with a bit of homework that I am not the only person who resists this area because of what might be living among that stuff. Like wolf spiders. Or brown recluses or black widows. Once I resisted clearing out my garage because I had seen a foot long alligator lizard (they bite) in there one day and I lived with the perpetual fear that a rattlesnake could slide under the door (which was not unreasonable). Maybe you need to set off a bug bomb before you tackle that room. Or get help. But eventually, tackle it. Have the proverbial garage sale. Call shelters and see if they will come pick stuff up. Above all, take your time. But get the job done.

When we are willing to do the work and put ourselves through these rigorous processes (which can be fun, actually) we and our environment begin to reflect a different kind of energy out to those around us. And the result will be a different kind of energy reflected back, be it in the form of a new friend, a new job, a new interest. Doors open, primarily because there is nothing blocking the way.

Last exercise. Go to the curb in front of your house (or wherever people begin to have access to you). Walk from the curb to your front door (or wherever people enter your house). Pay attention to everything that you come in contact with, or almost come in contact with. Are there branches reaching out? Leaves on the sidewalk? Plants falling over their natural boundaries? Or is it a pleasant flow from the first step to ringing the doorbell? Clip back. Sweep. Do it again. Use this as a metaphor throughout your process. What are you clearing away so everything that wants to come to you for your benefit can find you?

WHEN PULLING UP WEEDS
GET THE ROOT

I was shocked, frankly, when a high profile celebrity appeared on a major talk show recently announcing to the world at large, several million viewers, that the way she handled the stresses of her life was through "modern medicine". And she wasn't joking. She blithely saw meds as the answer to her lifestyle problem and that's clearly what she was advocating. My heart sank. She was a respected person, a fashion designer, being presented as one of America's powerful women, and a role model. I nearly wept thinking of the damage she was inadvertently doing. Could the drug companies have paid for any better advertising had they wanted to? I don't think so. I bet stocks soared that day.

It's not hard to see how this woman was sold this bill of goods. Every single night we are bombarded with the message to "ask our doctors" about the wonders of some drug. Worse, the primary message the drug companies are selling us is that it's not normal to have bad days or ups and downs, that we don't have time for such distractions, and that, why should we? Pop a pill. Been depressed for two weeks? Get a scrip. Who in the world hasn't been "depressed" for two weeks at some point in their lives? "Exactly," think the drug companies.

Life on planet Earth is a school. We're all enrolled. Problems are opportunities for nothing less than the soul's growth, for maturation, for development. Of course there are times when it's valid and important to seek a professional doctor's counseling and guidance and a drug might be an appropriate venue. And thank goodness for Novocain. But that's not what's happening. We are being told that rather than Doing the Work, take a drug. And that's dangerous territory. We take drugs rather than making the changes in our lifestyles that allow us to go to sleep naturally. We take drugs to stay awake, rather than getting the rest we need. We take drugs rather than simply monitoring our diets. We pop pills rather than learning the simple art of relaxation. We fill prescriptions that "allow us to avoid" our natural grief and pain. We buy drugs in order to have sex rather than exploring what that might really be about and drugs to have kids when our bodies would rather not. And we will take anything rather than experience old age. Have we totally lost all faith in an overall plan that is natural? Is everything something to be conquered with modern medicine? Is there no inkling that maybe someone or something greater than ourselves might be in charge and that the plan inherent in that scheme might be superior to anything we might imagine? Is there absolutely no surrender? No working in harmony? Only deals, deals, deals? And quick fixes?

We are becoming a drug addled culture. The War on Drugs needs to start in our own medicine cabinets, or by muting our tv's through certain sections of our evening news. Who invited these peddlers into our living rooms? Did you?

Emotional pain is not something we should be avoiding at all costs. Emotional pain and the daily stresses of life are critical messages from a highly complex and sophisticated and very *very* old system with which we are connected and wired. Any woman who has given birth will tell you this is true. Or, heck, good sex will tell you this. True spiritual experience will also tell you this but this is not something much sought after in our culture. Grief and pain are part of life to be experienced, not bypassed. Stress is a vital message that we probably need some lifestyle change. Angst is normal. It doesn't need to be masked. It needs to be listened to. And we need to respond.

Would you give a child a pill every time it cries? Of course not. Anyone who followed that procedure would be lambasted as a parent. Why is it socially acceptable to do it to ourselves? If some part of us is crying out, why would we not make the time to investigate, to delve, to honor that voice, that angst, that cry, that moan, that longing? Why would we take a pill and "make it go away"?

And what in the world does it do to the psyche to try to squelch these vital emotions?

It's true, our bodies are chemical structures on one level. We do have imbalances. We do need to correct them. What if correcting the imbalance meant taking a walk every day? Or meant getting more sleep? What if it meant seeing a grief counselor and experiencing the pain of some loss we had been avoiding for years? What if our lack of balance could be corrected by entering a yoga class and we found ourselves in a group of supportive, interesting women who became lifelong friends? When we are solving the "problems" we all are faced with, bypassing with medications is often not the correct response. Sometimes it's the perfect response, yes. But often the highest option is a natural, human and appropriate compassionate response, and very often, simply common sense. You're tired? Why are you sitting in front of the tv at 11:00 o'clock at night? Can you tivo Letterman? Go to bed! You have indigestion? Stop eating sugar and pizza! Find your self-love. Let that be your new drug.

What do you think your longings and your pains are trying to tell you? Do not drug them into oblivion. Open your hearts, your minds to your selves, your whole selves. It does you no good to mask these voices, these feelings. One must find the courage, the support, the means to find the center of the pain, to hearken to why it visits you and learn what it has to teach you. As you honor your process remind yourself there is an end, a letting go and a moving on. The tools you will need include bravery, support, a sense of humor, self-acceptance, compassion, forgiveness and a deep willingness to trust your feelings and what is behind them. Seek natural venues for your process, such as massage, herbs, counselors you have screened and trust. Trust your instincts. It is through this vital process that you reclaim your life as your own. You will open up a vital dialogue with yourself and strengthen who you are as a being. Don't be seduced into not claiming this, your earthly heritage. Know and trust that by going into the center, to the core, there lies a gift, a piece of work for your soul, wrapped in an unlikely package, one you do not readily move towards. Do not cheat yourself of the gift inherent in that offering. Gather courage, get support and move gently, willingly and persistently into the center of that which you resist. And move on. Lighter. Freer. Wiser.

TAKE HEART IN THE PLANT THAT SURVIVES ALL ODDS

On September 1, 2001 I made the somewhat rash decision that after thirty-five years in Northern California I was moving to Western North Carolina, sight unseen. Ten days later we were all stunned by 9-11. In the midst of planetary confusion I gathered up everything I treasured, had it loaded onto a truck and sent it off with a prayer. Virtual as the world has become, I had rented, by phone and fax, a house outside Asheville. It was set in the woods at the end of a dirt road, much as my home in California and the illusion of familiarity led me to believe I would know how to adapt readily. A week later I left with my Maine Coon showcat, Luna, and Sweet Pea, my deaf and semi-feral Siamese cat who had only two months before come to me out of the woods, and my faithful Border Collie, Peaches. I tearfully left behind my beloved

Bantam rooster, Chanticleer, whom I had rescued when he was lost in the woods, and his dear polka-dotted girlfriend, Henny Penny, with a neighbor who added them to her flock. I only allowed myself one plant: my ginkgo tree in a very large pot. All my roses, houseplants, etc. were left behind in the care of loving people. The tree had to come.

As fate would have it, I had unwittingly rented a house that I discovered to be full of toxic mold. Going through a national realtor and having a minister photograph the house for me (emailing me over thirty photos) could not have prepared me for this disaster. I will spare you the details. It's a book unto itself which I do not want to write. In the process of extracting myself from this highly toxic situation and securing a new clean and safe home in Asheville, I sorrowfully had little time and inclination to check on my beloved ginkgo tree. I myself was struggling to survive. The tree for now, at least, would have to wend its way on its own. Fortunately the soul memory of a ginkgo tree is very very old and if there's one thing a ginkgo tree knows how to do it's to survive. They are one of the oldest trees on the planet Earth.

I knew for a fact it had not been watered on the way, in spite of a request. As I reoriented myself to a new and very different culture, the tree sat patiently in the unpaved drive, deep in the woods of Appalachia, in the company of many forest trees who were steadfastly moving into the deep sleep of winter, as good trees do in colder climates. Would the ginkgo follow suit, or succumb to the rigors of single digit temperatures? Much as I loved that tree, my mind and heart were elsewhere, and I would longingly glance at it as I marched up and down a long stone staircase in my comings and goings in a courageous attempt to move us to another house. I wanted to do more, but what? I tried to allay my fears by recalling the history of ginkgo trees, hoping this young tree would remember its longevity and somehow miraculously survive. For the moment I had to leave it to its fate and secure my own.

I remember how comforted I felt once my ginkgo was standing resolutely on the back deck of the new house. I knew the lines of those branches, and they now stood just outside my kitchen window, offering familiarity and a declaration of victory secured. We were safe. But had it really survived, or would I be staring into the thin long branches of what once was, yet another token of what I'd left behind, what I'd lost in the great risk of such a monumental undertaking?

I fretted over this and poked around at the tree, testing its branches periodically for flexibility, nibbling at it with shears to uncover some hint of something living. Nothing for sure. Was that a touch of green, or was that left over from a life once lived? I took the route of skeptical optimism, a certain oxymoron. I covered the pot with a blanket during the next big freeze after a gentle Southern man in a decrepit nursery on a back country road had listened quietly to my concern over this tree and reminded me that pots do not offer roots the same protection as surefooted trees in the ground. A good metaphor resounding with teardrops in my heart, not lost on me for a second.

One cold morning in March I surveyed this tree once again and I reluctantly got out the pruning shears again, needing desperately to know. Clipped a branch. Clipped a bud. Cut. Cut. Imagine my heart, my joy when at last I found within a dried up crusty old bud a leaf. Yes, a leaf, curled up ever so tightly, but ever so alive within this hard dry casing! No mistaking life, my friend. No mistaking life.

At this fragile juncture of my journey this seemingly small event was for me a huge sign that we had survived this winter phase of our lives. We were rolled up tightly, but inside was the green leaf of life, yet to unfold, yet to show our true colors and flourish. How I blessed this little ginkgo tree, and, oh, how I took heart.

Dear friend, do take heart in the plant that survives all odds.

JUDGE NOT THE FLOWER BY ITS BUD

Shortly after moving to my new home in North Carolina I discovered a bleeding heart plant growing in between the bushes in front of the house. I recognized it as a shade-loving plant and happily transplanted it to a shady corner behind the house. As the little flowers emerged I was struck with disappointment and nostalgia, as these were not the same flowers I had come to love in California, the ones I knew well, the ones I had bought in nurseries at home. Two weeks later my heart filled with joy as I stumbled upon a nursery tucked below the road I had taken on errands, and outside in the various lovely displays I found another bleeding heart, with the very flowers that I associated with my home state. Delighted, I purchased it immediately, going straight home to plant it in a big clay pot I'd found on sale the week before.

Imagine my surprise when the following week I walked through the shade garden and found the little flowers I had snubbed the week before were identical to the ones I had just bought. Apparently I had never seen a bleeding heart in bud before, always opting to buy fully mature versions in nurseries, never having grown them from seed.

I laughed at myself, realizing I had judged the flower by its bud, indeed, had not even recognized it as a bud! I began to wonder how many times I might have judged some creative effort, either my own or someone else's, in the same manner. How many times have we encountered a fledgling effort and rejected it as not good enough, as a waste of time or as stupid? When had we been willing to bring forth the virtues of patience and close observation, and allowed the time to pass for full maturation, we might have found that what we first thought unacceptable grew to the loveliest of flowers that sustained us for many years.

DISTINGUISH FRIENDS
FROM PREDATORS

I think the first person who told me there were rattlesnakes on our mountain in Santa Rosa was my German neighbor down below, also a Hall, whom she married. She even had a daughter named Kathryn Hall and a daughter-in-law named Kathryn Hall. That's, in fact, how I met her. Sears delivered a lawnmower I had ordered to her house instead of to mine. Apparently they had a wooden sign out in front of their small farm that said Hall and the driver saw it and thought it was me. She accepted it, thinking her daughter-in-law had purchased it for her son as a surprise. Later the mistake was caught, the mower rightfully was delivered to me and so we became friends, the kind that literally talk over the backyard fence, and this is how I learned that there were rattlesnakes. I was none too keen to learn this. She took it in stride, as she had lived on that mountain since she was a bride, and killing rattlesnakes I guess came with the territory, especially if you raised hens, which she used to do. She said the snakes liked to curl up inside woodpiles, a fact that made carting wood from outside to the woodstove an onerous task ever after. I never did see a snake in there, but I did see many a scorpion, which is not as bad, but scary nonetheless.

The German woman laughed when she saw how frightened I guess I appeared when she told me matter of factly that you kill rattlesnakes with a shovel. I tried to imagine, but could not. The sheer thought of killing any snake was more than I could fathom. Not me. I wondered if I would ever become like this woman who had taken this for granted as one of the prices one paid for living on that hill. I didn't think so.

Later I happened to discuss this conversation with the postmistress and she laughed, herself a country woman. "Oh, yes," she smiled. "And this is what you do." She stood back a bit, obviously holding an imaginary shovel and thrust it out hard in front of her toward the ground. "Flip it over. Like this. And then, hard, whack their heads off. And then bury the head. Always bury the head."

I shivered. "Why?" I asked.

"Because the head will keep moving, and it can still bite. It's where the poison is, and you need to keep it away from other animals. Do you have dogs or cats? Both? OK, then put it deep in the ground so they can't get to it. So no animal will smell it and dig it up."

I drove home somberly, wondering what I would do if I came across such a snake, wondering if I could ever find it in myself to do what these women had accessed within themselves and took for granted.

I had heard a horror story from a woman I knew about the sister of a friend who lived up a little further north in wine country who had found her young son playing near a rattlesnake. Her mother instincts kicked in and she hurriedly scooped up her son to safety and ran for a shovel which she levied down on the snake's head. Unfortunately her upper body strength was lacking and the blow did not sever the head—it merely pinned down the snake. To this day I find it hard to imagine the courage it took for that woman to lift the shovel off the head of that writhing snake in order to deal the second fatal blow, rendering her son and herself safe.

As it happened, there were, indeed, rattlesnakes about my home. The first one I saw when one of my dogs was barking out front and I went to investigate. A rattler was coiled up only a few feet from my front door, gearing to strike at my dog. I called my dog to me and she obeyed. That snake got away.

After that I bought a sturdy flatheaded shovel and always kept it leaning against the house, wondering if I would ever need to use it, and hoping I never would. In point of fact seeing rattlers became more common the longer I lived there, a fact I always attributed to the incessant building that took place on that mountain, destroying habitat of not only rattlesnakes but also every other critter that lived among us. It chilled me to learn rattlers hibernated in dens with up to a dozen snakes, or more, though it interested me to know they shared their dens with snakes not of their own kind.

I researched what their predators are, thinking that if perhaps I introduced some of their predators I could keep their numbers down if not at bay. Mongoose and peacocks were not likely pets. Kingsnakes eat them and there were kingsnakes about, but not in the numbers that were needed. A man I knew who had lived on that hill insisted that if I had a couple of barn cats I wouldn't feed they would eat enough mice that no snake would have a reason to come, but I could not bring myself to own such an outdoor cat.

I was made of other stuff.

When rattlesnakes did show up I did what women from time immemorial have done. I went and got a man. Mostly I went next door and called on my neighbor Ray, a full block from my house, but willing to come and do the dirty deed. When snakes came I prayed that he would be home and then I prayed the snake would still be where I found it when I returned with help.

Often there was some drama involved. One snake I found in my front garden and my little Henny Penny had her foot precisely next to the snake's head, almost touching it. Yelling at her did no good. I had to throw a rock at her to get her to move. She flew into the air with a start and I feared the move would start a chain reaction and I would lose the snake, but no. It stood its ground. I got Ray.

Ray came another time when an extremely large rattlesnake, a full three feet long, became tangled in a piece of garden netting I had left next to the pool, planning to store it later. That snake was so frightened and so angry, struggling in the net, trying to free itself. I felt sorry for it. Again Ray saved the day.

One Saturday afternoon I was helping my Mexican gardeners clear deep grasses from around the house, to keep a defensible space for fire protection and as I leaned over to pull up a large bunch I found myself looking straight at the back of a large rattlesnake napping at the base of the grasses. I alerted my gardeners and they ran like excited boys to see. Now I saw the Mexican version, how you kill a snake in Michaocan. They calmly found a branch from a tree that had a fork at the end. They moved quietly and fearlessly toward the snake, focused, their adrenaline rushing. They put the fork over the snake's head, pinning it down, and then used the shovel. They put the head in a plastic bag. That head opened its mouth for the next half hour and I saw clearly what that postmistress had been telling me. They *can* still bite.

Periodically I would pick up the flatheaded shovel and plunge it toward the ground, practicing for the day maybe Ray or my gardeners would not be there to help me out.

My initiation into killing snakes came one afternoon when I saw a baby rattler next to the guesthouse. I could not afford to have a baby snake near me or my animals, especially as it's the babies that throw the most venom. I felt I could do this. I picked up the flatheaded shovel and thrust it down on the snake's head. I had killed my first snake. It was not long after that I literally tripped over another baby and I realized there must be a den close by. I killed this one as well. Two.

I don't think I had occasion to kill another snake in my remaining time in California. I knew I had begun to integrate a survivor skill that I would not be apt to need, but felt empowered somewhat to know I was beginning to find that in myself and to be able to act.

Not long after I arrived in North Carolina I heard my neighbor next door calling hysterically that her wirehaired terrier had found a snake. Apparently the dog had found it hiding and had pulled it out from some rocks. She kept shouting over and over in her deep Southern accent, "Izzy has a snake! Izzy has a snake!" Her son had come with a shovel and I could see him stabbing at the snake. Instinctively I rushed up steps to their backyard. "Give me the shovel!" I commanded. The son, confused, passed me the shovel. I saw a familiar pattern on the back of the snake and without thinking I flipped over the shovel and chopped off his head.

This was my full introduction to my new neighbors. A near stranger barging into their backyard and chopping off the head of a snake. Nice.

What ensued was an after-the-fact discussion of what kind of snake I had just killed. As it turned out it was a harmless garden snake who eats bugs and keeps the garden in balance, and I felt terribly guilty, but not sorry I had done what I did.

I only saw one snake after that in North Carolina. I was in the back garden pulling weeds when a small black snake slithered out from under the ivy. The snake deliberately eyed me and I deliberately eyed the snake, sizing him up. I decided he was harmless and he decided he would keep an eye on me as he made his escape. I asked him to leave and not come back. I watched as he slinked into the thick undergrowth on the other side of the fence and I never saw him again.

In assessing whether a being is friend or foe I think back often to a small black woman my daughter and I met outside the Marin County Courthouse, where the woman was visiting her husband who was in jail. As we spoke the woman rolled her eyes as she climbed into the back of a red pickup truck, her ride home. "One thing I can tell you, children, is know who you're foolin' with. Un huh. Know who you're foolin' with."

Indeed.

PLAN YOUR ACTIVITIES IN HARMONY WITH THE SEASONS

One morning during the two years I lived in North Carolina I was taking books down off a shelf and as I did so, one book fell open to a particular page which caught my attention. The book was therapist Natalie Rogers' *Emerging Woman*, and the chapter I was staring at was titled "Uprooting and Rerooting". I found this very apropos for a woman who had pulled herself up from many years of living in Northern California transplanting herself into a rain forest called Appalachia. No accident whatsoever. I read on. As it happened, Natalie had lived for a similar period in Connecticut and had transplanted herself to Northern California. What intrigued me most was Natalie's insight that by coordinating the timing of her transplantation with her last child's leaving the nest, Natalie could possibly avoid some of the pangs that invariably come with being an empty nester. So as the daughter was leaving, Natalie was also. One of her goals in so doing, apparently, was to reduce the risk that she might fall into a pattern of waiting, something she had heard and seen other empty nest mothers do. As an empty nester myself, I could imagine. As one's grown child leaves home a mother naturally feels deep angst as her role is changing. When that child comes home to visit the Mom gets her familiar role back. She prepares for the visit, getting the house ready, the garden ready, the cupboards full, the fridge or cookie jar full, etc. Child visits. Child leaves. Mom is in a rut again. She falls into the pattern of waiting. For primarily in the planning for the return can mom find herself active in the familiar role of mother. She gets her job back. It was illuminating for me to see how waiting for the child could be so seductive to a mom, rather than to take the bigger risk of looking to see what has been waiting for her on a closet shelf since the day her child was born, or when she found out she was pregnant, or decided she wanted to get pregnant. What was appropriate then—to put other dreams on hold, and to focus exclusively on the dream of being a parent—may not be appropriate once the children are gone.

What is it that is waiting for you until the perfect season? Will you be able to leave the comfort of long held roles and seek out what you put behind until you could return to it again? Perhaps now is the time, the perfect time, to plan your activities in harmony with your *own* inner seasons.

INVITE A FRIEND TO
KEEP YOU COMPANY

It was the Fourth of July and how would I celebrate? I had not made plans. My family was far away in California and Utah. I wasn't a big Fourth of July fan anyway unless I was at a big fireworks display at night with friends and I hadn't done that in a long time. I could hear that my neighbors had company, no doubt from their native Arkansas, and they had the barbeque fired up and I felt a pang of loneliness. I allowed it to move through as a cloud crossing the sky blocking the light of the sun for a brief moment. The sun reemerged as I allowed and let go.

Some weeks before I had been glancing out onto the side deck outside my office at dusk and something had caught my eye in the tree. A lump. What could it be? Some part of me knew it to be a bird, but my logical mind sought to make it a squirrel, as it seemed too large to be any common bird in North Carolina in a pine tree just outside my office in a somewhat urban area. But I knew it was not a squirrel. What then? What lump on a branch in a tree just before nightfall? Two lumps, actually. Then three. Then four. A stunning realization dawned. Owls! Four owls! How could I be looking at four owls? I've been on the planet a long time. I have never seen four owls, but I was seeing them now.

In the days that followed a flurry of research was set off, including dialogues with Audubon folk and email with a raptor guy in Charlotte. Yes, they are around. No, they are not often seen. I discover they are Eastern Screech Owls. They came back to the tree in twos, in threes, or alone. They came nightly for over a week. Then they were gone. Fledged?

Three weeks later they started to return in the evening. Never four, however. Never four.

My yoga teacher Melissa stopped by. I told her about them. I showed her. "There?" she said, incredulously. "Here? This close? Right here?" Yes, fifteen feet away, in the lower branches of my trees, they came. They clearly recognized me and they trusted me. "What are they here to tell you?" she asked. I think they are here to keep me company. They are here to make me feel less alone.

Not long after Melissa left I went out on the deck, and found myself slightly adjusting the furniture so that all four chairs on the deck were now around a central table. The subtle guidance for this adjustment was not lost on me. Four is the number of structure. It is building. It is foundation. It is solidity. It is intentional and it is inviting.

Influence (Wooing):
Thus the superior man encourages people to approach him
By his readiness to receive them.
The I Ching

I had no idea what it would bring, but I knew it was the right thing to do. I went back inside and looked out on the deck, contented. It was good.

At dusk on the Fourth of July, two days later, I am looking to see if any of my owls are in the trees. I step back, startled. They are in the rafters of my deck, six feet above my head, and they are four.

I spend the next hour and a half giggling, speaking gently to them, smiling, sending them the most welcoming, safe and inclusive energy I can broadcast to them. They clearly know me. I take a bold step. I get my camera. I know in my gut it is OK. I ever so gently slide back the screen door, just enough to get a clear view of them from my camera lens. I snap. I snap again. I close the screen carefully and breathe. I wait. I open and snap again. My energy is gentle, respectful, humble, honored, thrilled.

They are sitting in perfect symmetry. Two above on the highest beam, and one to each side, perfectly, perfectly symmetrical. This is no accident. This is a moment in time.

I sit quietly with them for over an hour. I watch everything I can.

Two seem to be parents, two babies. I watch, utterly enchanted, as a baby moves towards the one I imagine to be the mother and reaches out with his claw, nudging her. Preen me, he's saying. She preens. The baby tucks its head down near the feet of the mama owl making his head ever so available, convenient. My heart pours out in gratitude to be witnessing this intimate, exquisite exchange. The mother burrows her beak gently into his neck. She nuzzles him. I am in awe watching what I feel few have watched, what I have certainly never watched. Four owls above my head in the rafters.

The rufus-colored baby silently moves out onto a branch of a nearby tree, just beyond the deck. He is in much better light and I stretch my capacity to follow each line of his soft downy feathers intertwined with impossibly tiny white feathers that trace downward to his strong pointed beak. I try to look with new eyes as I have never looked before. I painstakingly note the roundness of the top of his head and the million tiny variegated feathers that make up his outer body as he lifts his head skyward to something which catches his attention, his eyelids slipping halfway over his large yellow eyes and the large black pupils. This is the most charming bird I have ever seen. I feel blessed beyond measure to be in the company of these owls and to be honored with their trust. I give thanks to them and for this moment in time that I will treasure for a lifetime. I allow myself to wonder ever so briefly just how much longer such an experience will be possible on planet Earth? I pray for their survival and well being. I pray we as a species will access and use our wisdom to make this moment possible for centuries to come, pray that this will not be a rare and fleeting experience.

Gradually one by one and slowly over the space of the next half an hour, they exit the stage of my rafters into the greenery adjacent to my deck. One on a branch. One quickly out of sight. Finally the mother, the last, moves to a long branch that gives me a very clear view of her entire body in the light. And then they were gone. Fireflies begin to take their place in the landscape. My attention moves quietly to their luminescent presence in the garden air.

What an extraordinary and quiet Fourth of July, and what an unexpected celebration of life!

What is it we invite in to share our time, our attention? What kindles our joy, our compassion? What makes the moment immeasurably rich? How do we set the stage for such experiences to come to us? And how are our hearts nurtured by the company we each keep, each of us choosing our own paths, and how does the transformation that comes with that choice enhance not only our own lives but those of others?

Invite a friend to keep you company.

TEST AND AMEND YOUR SOIL

In the garden the most basic of basics is to know the qualities of the soil in which you are growing your plants. In North Carolina I found the soil to be quite hard and rocky and containing a lot of clay. In the mountains of Northern California the soil is rich and fragrant, also quite rocky, and a joy to work with. It is full of life and plants spring forth from it readily. Undoubtedly the vast quantities of rain, the abundant sunshine and the proximity to the sea contribute mightily to the quality of the soil there. And in North Carolina which is known for its great plant diversity, the elements of extreme dampness and of shorter summers play a large part in determining the nature of its soil.

If we were to evaluate the soil in which we find ourselves as living beings we would have several lenses through which we might look, including the cultures in which we plant ourselves, as well as the nutrients we choose to give ourselves upon which we thrive.

As I have moved about, transplanting myself into various cultures, each has significantly contributed to the sum total of who I am today and for all those peoples and places I am very grateful. I thank the Dutch for teaching me more tolerance. I thank the Mexicans for showing me deep compassion, a warm hospitality and heartful support. I am grateful to Southerners for demonstrating their graciousness. I thank the culture of California for encouraging me to be more fully myself and for the vast numbers of wonderful teachers I have come across. I thank Puerto Ricans for showing me their deep humility and faith. I thank the French for showing me style. I thank the Germans for their inquisitiveness, their thoroughness and their insightfulness. I thank New Englanders for showing me the value of family rootedness and tradition. Every place has something to teach us. Each shapes and molds us and makes us who we are becoming.

I will never forget one evening sitting around a fire with perhaps a couple dozen folks at a Kite Festival in Holland at which we were all camping. As it so happened the people around that circle were from all over the globe. A friend and I were quietly observing the various couples and we noted with fascination and humor that the Europeans tended to be sitting close together speaking quietly, respecting the others in the group, while the Americans and Australians were boldly expressing themselves back and forth across the fire one side to the other, calling out with no seeming regard for the others in the circle and how they might be impacting their reality. In thinking about this we realized that the Americans and Australians both came from large territories where a real concern for sharing space with others was not always a necessary consideration.

Soil does matter.

Our thoughts and beliefs also contribute to the "soil" in which we grow. Yet how aware are we of our core beliefs and the very thoughts we feed ourselves on a daily basis that are determining the culture in which we live and grow? What might we be missing? As famed trainer Werner Erhard used to ask, "How do you know that you don't know what you don't know?"

And how do you find out?

Do we marinate ourselves in negative thinking and expect to thrive? Is our inner critic out of control? Do we take breaks throughout the day changing our pace to integrate, reframe and recuperate, or do we reach for another cup of coffee and push our way through the day on caffeine and adrenaline? Do we congratulate ourselves on our accomplishments or do we see only what could have been better? Do we indulge in comparison, judgments and water cooler gossip or do we stand steadfast in support of our colleagues? Do we turn to prayer, visualization, journaling and reflection or turn on the tv or computer and drown out our own internal wisdom?

Ultimately the soil we are obliged to test and amend is our very own thinking. It is in this process that you will reclaim your own intrinsic power and glory and beauty and become the lovely special you that you are here to be.

ALLOW AMPLE SPACE FOR THE
BREADTH OF YOUR VISION

There was a particular woman in my yoga class in North Carolina who was a fabulous role model for aging. She was petite, very active, fit and quite attractive. She took very good care of her body. After yoga I always admired that she was usually off to the weight room. I was surprised to learn that she was nearly seventy and that she had just gone through the protracted illness of her husband, who subsequently passed away. Shortly after learning this I happened to run into her while shopping and she invited me to join her and her friend for lunch. I looked forward to this opportunity to get to know her better. I learned she was from the South, and, indeed, I had always thought of her as a very charming Southern lady in the highest sense. There's a certain breed of Southern woman who always seems to know the right thing to say at the right moment. Ever charming and gracious with a delightful sense of humor, always able to smooth any social situation, regardless of the circumstance. This woman was of that sophisticated schooling and I found her fascinating. As the conversation deepened and we began to ask questions of each other in earnest, she divulged to me some of the details of her husband's long illness. And here she was emerged on the other side, her children grown, with the rest of her life before her. I saw a wide door opening. She had never lived alone. She had always framed her life around the needs of her husband and children. I began to ask her about her dreams. Were there places she wanted to go? Places she had never seen she now had the opportunity to visit? It had not been long since I had met a woman in her seventies at the airport who was on her way to Thailand by herself. She had said her family did not understand but that she wanted to see the world and she was comfortable traveling to many places. I was imagining such an answer.

"Well," she drawled slowly, hesitantly, "I've always wanted to see Montana." Pause. "And Utah?"

I was stunned. I smiled. "Montana?" I queried.

"Yes," she answered demurely.

Mind you, Montana is a lofty destination. It offers unparalleled, unspoiled beauty. But here before me was a woman with her life opening up before her totally unfettered and the furthest her imagination could reach in that moment was a short plane ride away. It was not for me to judge. Perhaps this was the perfect avenue for her. Perhaps after Montana her appetite would be whetted and she would take a tour and go to, say, Ireland? You can bet that before the end of our afternoon together I did my best to mirror for her that she was at an enviable crossroads of opportunity. She said she had never looked at it like that before. Whew!

There is a large red banner across my frig that I cut from my car insurance newsletter. It says in bold white letters, "It's your planet. See it!" I love that message scrawled across my daily reverie.

How large a canvas do you need on which to paint your life? Might it be contained within a small town? A thriving metropolis? Two continents? An island? All of the above? In what languages is it written? How many? In what schools are you enrolled? What congregations? In which families are you engaged? How large a stage does your soul need to play its part in this lifetime? Do your imagination and creativity work in concert allowing sufficient space, texture, nuance and substance to fully express all of who you really are?

TRIM UNWIELDY BRANCHES

The unwieldy branches in our gardens are usually quite obvious. They demand our attention as we try to move about and we get poked in the eye or smacked in the face. Ordinarily, though not always, we get out the tree sheers and cut these annoying branches back, and we are free to walk about the garden unencumbered. This trimming not only assists us in our freedom of movement, it allows the tree to direct its resources to the vital, central parts of itself, engendering a longer, healthier and more vigorous life.

In North Carolina it is not uncommon to see large fragmented branches suspended precariously from the tops of stately trees, broken off by a fierce wind passing through, that was not quite strong enough to bring the branch down. They dangle in the balance waiting to come crashing through the branches below, possibly on our heads. For these situations we are likely to call a tree service and request that they assist in removing the danger. It's a simple enough task.

How so in our personal lives? What are the unwieldy branches that cause our days to be prickly affairs rather than a smooth flow? At the other extreme, are there branches suspended dangerously over our heads (or that's how it feels anyway) that might come crashing down at any moment? What to do?

Two good grids for evaluating such hazards, large or small, can be found in taking a look at our overextensions and incompletions. We all have them. Essentially what we want to do is to manage our own energies more efficiently by eliminating energetic distractions that get in our way and keep us from operating at peak performance. Sounds great, doesn't it?

Some energetic drains are found in rigorously established patterns that are so habitual we take them for granted and it never occurs to us to make a change. A good example would be picking up the mail at the post office and carting all of it to the car, taking it home and putting it on the kitchen counter and getting to it later. The flip side paradigm would be to take the mail out of the box, processing it while standing in line to buy stamps, or, putting the mail on the post office table and doing a first pass right then and there, and then tossing all the junkmail in the post office recycling bin. You are halfway through your mail. You've already recycled. It took two minutes. When you get home all personal mail goes in one place and all business mail goes in another.

Other examples include having the kids make their own lunches in the evening rather than your squeezing in this task each morning. Or taking the time to organize a carpool to take the kids to lessons or to school. These simple shifts make a difference on your energy, and that's what we are trying to preserve.

What about The Little Things? Little things that you have not managed to get to are like mini energy sappers. They are literally distracting you (even if you think you have put them "out of your mind") and keeping you from being the streamlined machine you need to be. Think of swimmers who shave their bodies because their body hair will slow them down. Often whatever is forever rattling around in your brain that you haven't gotten to yet is simply an incomplete action. What would it take to complete it?

"Push it through," a girlfriend of mine once told me in the Sixties, up in the woods of Sonoma County when I was surveying my room full of clutter and I was feeling overwhelmed and very whiney. Simple, but profound words. I knew what to do. I got to work. One piece at a time. I got it.

Now I am in the habit of always fitting these seemingly "off purpose" tasks into my daily workflow. When I neglect them they are out on the periphery asking for my attention, siphoning off my energy from where I want it. And the amazing thing that I witness over and over again is that the amount of time it takes to actually do some of these little annoying energy drains is usually a minute. And when I compare that teeny investment of my time and energy to the space this task was holding over my being, I am in awe of how counter productive it was for me not to finish it sooner.

Years ago I got a call from a woman I knew who wanted to hire me to help her "organize" a catch-all room she had filled up to the point she felt paralyzed into inaction. We sat there together. I picked up one thing after another. Where do you recycle your papers? Where do you store old bills? Where is your trash? It wasn't that she couldn't manage the individual decisions. She had all the answers. It was that the task had grown to such proportion that the enormity of it was overwhelming. She literally needed me to pick up one thing after another and ask her where it went. So sometimes we call the tree service, the troops, the bookkeeper, the housekeeper, the babysitter. We are human. We are fragile. We are not designed to be good at *everything*. We need help.

What are the unwieldy branches showing up in your life? What are the silent phantoms that rob you of your precious energy? How does that make you feel? What would a more streamlined, energized version of yourself look and feel like and what do you need to do to bring that into reality?

PLANT SUN-LOVING PLANTS
IN THE SUN; PLANT SHADE-LOVING
PLANTS IN THE SHADE

One evening during my daughter's visit to North Carolina she stepped outside into the chilly night air and back in again, asking, "Mom, what's that sound in the trees? What animal?" I couldn't really tell her. I'd seen them. Large, dark, winged bugs that, frankly, don't appeal. I just didn't know their name.

"They are cicadas," a woman jogging by my house one afternoon informed me. I read about them. They spend years underground, emerging to mate and it's the male that Webster's says "produces a shrill sound by means of vibrating membranes on the underside of its abdomen". The female cicada recognizes this staccato song as a call to creation.

A week later, as I lay on an acupuncture table, I sat up excitedly when I thought I heard a frog in the room, and laughed when I realized it was a CD that my Chinese acupuncturist had decided to play, to help create a calming atmosphere. I lay back down and was suddenly overcome with a flood of nostalgia and longing for my beloved Pacific Coast treefrogs in Santa Rosa that lived in all my flower pots, my own little secret garden angels that, if you were very lucky and very special I would share with you when you came to visit.

"Look," I'd whisper, gently lifting up a large pot off its saucer on the deck and several tiny bright green iridescent creatures would scurry for safety into the shade and moisture of anything they could find in which to hide. Oh, how I loved them, and do. For me they were the little secret fairy creatures who lived amongst my life. I was ceaselessly enchanted by them. No one ever knew they were there, but me. They hid behind the flower boxes of cyclamen and azaleas that lined the deck, down inside the cymbidium pots, along the edges of saucers of Sweet Williams and a random lantana. They were part of my secret world. Occasionally I would pick them up ever so carefully and put them on the flat of my hand or on my arm and watch with sheer fascination and delight, and they would sit in their innocence of having been lifted from one reality to the next, until I would gently lower my arm to the ground and they would hop back into their familiar world, where they belonged.

At night instead of the grating of cicadas I would open the windows to the choirs of crickets and pond frogs who lived in huge abundance about my home, and their songs lulled me into deep and satisfying slumber. In North Carolina I crack my window as little as possible to allow in air, but muffle the ratcheting cicadas who impose upon my dreamstate summer and fall and make me wonder where I am. Soon winter will come and their cacophony will blessedly disappear as they apparently make their way back into the lightless tunnels from which they emerged.

People who grew up in Appalachia have a fierce and abiding love of these mountains. The cicadas sang their lullabies to them in constancy as children. It is what they know and what they love and long for when they leave. I run into people repeatedly who left Appalachia only to return years later, longing for the simple charm and comfort of home, of familiarity, of reliability, of slow and little traffic, for the warmth of the soothing Southern drawl, for the abiding presence of these ancient mountains from which they draw strength and nurturance. They speak to them. Myths abound of the mystic healing qualities the Appalachian mountains offer. "You've come to heal," locals told me. Maybe. I'm more of a mind that healing exists in every opportunity, regardless of where we are. However it is certain that the mountains of Appalachia have a rich and varied history of early resorts and inns geared solely to the rejuvenation of those who visited, and perhaps it is out of this early intention that these stories spring.

As the cheerful sunflower thrives in the sun's harsh rays, so the gentle foxglove flourishes in the protection of the forest floor. We must be where we belong to bring out the best in us. Adventures are good. They are expanding. Ultimately we must listen to the voice in our hearts that takes us to the place where we thrive and relate and call our sacred home.

Where is it you know you belong? Are you there? If so, glory be and, oh, give thanks daily. If not, what would it take to move towards that place that calls to you, that nurtures you, that recognizes you as one of their own, and whom you recognize as your own tribe? What is it that ultimately determines who and what bears heart and meaning for you and is there anything you need to heed to quicken your steps and heart in that direction?

REFRAME ALL ERROR AS LEARNING

My grandmother always told me it was because of when my birthday fell, in spring, that I entered first grade a year younger than my peers. Back then probably not much was made of placing a child so much younger than her classmates in the same class. Maybe if I'd been bigger it would not have mattered much. But as it happened, I was not only the youngest, but the smallest child in the classroom. Add to this the fact that I was rather pigeon-toed and you do not have a child apt to do well on the playground. (Not unless you count jacks and marbles.) Add to this my terror at being placed inside a circle with half my classmates while the other half stood on the edge throwing a large hard ball at me which I was supposed to "dodge". And this was supposed to be a fun thing. It is not hard to imagine that when teams were formed for any kind of sport I was the last to be chosen, and there were loud complaints, as most children are wont to make, about having to have me on their team.

This situation does not lend itself to learning sports in an even-handed secure manner. No, this actually leads to what we might call arrested development.

Piecemeal attempts were made to remedy my situation, though only the symptoms were addressed, as is still often the case with modern medicine. Under the advice of a well-intentioned doctor, I was forced to wear my shoes on the wrong feet, and I was put into ballet classes as the fundamental ballet position is toes pointed outward. And so my foundation began to change, in a rather haphazard way.

I did finally learn to ride a bike, and to skate, which I found quite thrilling. But this entire area of being in charge of moving things requiring coordination remained sketchy at best for many years, and deeply affected my willingness to learn things that required any kind of physical challenge, where I might hurt myself or, worse, feel humiliated. This might help to explain why I did not get a driver's license until I was 31 years old.

I dragged this baggage with me to San Francisco in the late Sixties, where I was exposed to Eastern thought that was making its way through the culture at the time, and the Buddhist concept of Beginner Mind was introduced to me. This state of mind, which one must consciously cultivate, encourages one to approach each situation with the fresh eyes of a beginner, recognizing that one never steps into the same river twice in the same way, that each moment provides a new opportunity for a different outcome. Learning for me began to take on a new context, that of spiritual discipline. I became mindful of my thoughts, and of regulating my thoughts. Most importantly, I became aware that there was a connection between my thoughts and my external reality.

As I became more conscious of my internal dialogue, I became increasingly aware of various distinct voices within that dialogue, and noticed that those voices did not always agree. Further inspection revealed that some of them were archetypal, and Jean Shinoda Bolen's book *Goddesses in Everywoman* assisted me in recognizing who within me might be speaking. Her emphasis was on the various archetypal goddesses (Hestia, the one who tends the hearth; Aphrodite, the sensuous one; Athena, the one who is good at critical thinking).

Simultaneously there was another body of information emerging in our culture that allowed folks to begin to isolate and identify some of the other archetypal voices we find within our selves, including the Inner Child and the Inner Critic. This work was made available to the public largely through two important PBS series, one focusing on therapist John Bradshaw's work with understanding family systems and the other Bill Moyers' interviews with intellectual Joseph Campbell.

It was my great good fortune in North Carolina to live only a block from a lovely well appointed gym, part of a marvelous old mountain resort. There I studied yoga and swam several times each week. As I am a very early riser, I had the distinct advantage of arriving at this gym almost before anyone else, giving me the luxury of a large indoor pool nearly all to myself. This gave me the opportunity to re-explore my relationship to my body in water in the most unencumbered way, without any sort of social pressure or distraction. Slowly I found my way to being fully comfortable in the water, for the first time in my life. Each morning I navigated and explored the various ways I could arrive from pool's edge to opposite pool's edge at whatever pace I chose. I could challenge myself as I watched the clock, or I could glide slowly, smoothly, effortlessly over the water's surface and back again, often chanting out loud.

My water world expanded. I purchased my own little webby high tech gloves that gave me a new sensation as I swam. I found myself to be a different creature; a duck, or perhaps a swan. There was no critic there. There were no errors. No competition unless I chose it, against my own self. Only the quiet joy and thrill of self discovery and learning.

CLEAN UP AFTER A STORM

One unsuspecting autumn, in the space of five minutes, more than one hundred mature and stately trees came crashing down in Asheville, North Carolina. They came barreling into eaves of roofs, roofs themselves, into cars and yards, and across streets and power lines, grinding neighborhoods into an unexpected and shocking halt. Massive root systems lay bare and exposed, their tangled life severed from years of dedicated and steady service in a flash.

I had been on the phone, talking to a client, glanced out the window and noticed the Japanese crabtree branches lashing about uncharacteristically, made a small mental note and turned my attention back to the conversation at hand. When I hung up the phone moments later everything was curiously still. It was not until I left the house shortly after to run afternoon errands that I realized that in those five short minutes seemingly all of life shifted to revolve around the aftermath of the devastation that mysterious and seemingly harmless brief wind had left behind.

Then spring. I am standing on the porch. In an hour's time the temperatures have catapulted downward. What was rain moments before now lacquers trees with ice and burdens them with the heavy weight of an unexpected snow. The branches of the flowering crabapple tree that survived the lashing winds of fall are lowering their extended arms closer and closer to the ground, hearty red buds trustingly now encrusted with the white of snow, a strange sight to a California girl. I stand in the freezing cold, poised and helpless, waiting almost breathless, for the inevitable crashing of branches. My heart is breaking in knowing they will fall. Craaaackk, crash. Craaaaack, crash. All about the neighborhood, even as the snow offers the softening of all sound, the continuous cracking and crashing comes from all directions. Large branches with leaves burgeoning, no longer streamlined to endure such weight, succumb to the fast falling snowfall and come streaking through the trees to the ground, hitting sister trees and branches as they fall. My heart grieves with each break and resounding descent as I track their demise.

And so it is sometimes.

Unexpected events enter and depart and leave us suddenly broken, shapeless, collapsed, immobile, and hurting. And in both cases the solution in the same. We must clean up after the storm.

Cleaning up after a personal storm can mean many things. Sometimes it entails the primary expressions of rage, anger or sorrow, depending on the ferocity and impact of the storm. This step is generally not to be skipped, and to cause no further ill will to self or others must be done in the most conscientious, constructive ways. These strong emotions are not to be used as instruments to hurt either self or others. Rather these feelings need to be experienced and released, not unlike the falling of a rain on the receptive Earth. Express. Release. Let go. And now forgive, even if you are not quite ready to forget. Forgive yourself first, for being part of this unexpected event, and then begin to forgive those with whom you danced this sad and angry dance.

Having released the emotional charge of a personal storm, one can move on to restorative healing. This process is not necessarily a linear path, though I myself am apt to literally make a list of the resources I have at hand and begin to work my way through that list, going where I feel most drawn. To gentle massage. To healing acupuncture. To a nurturing spa, which one can often access just for the day. To being out of doors. To yoga. To swimming. To walking around the lake. To deep restorative slumber, allowing Spirit to work things out a bit in our dreams.

I provide myself with food I know will act as high powered fuel, which is what I need. I do not generally use food for comfort any longer. I know that giving myself the best fuel around is going to move me much faster to where I want (and deserve) to be. By the same token I do not lambaste myself or take myself to task if I eat some little sweet. You will not, however, find me standing in front of an open refrigerator door looking for a fix. I know it isn't there.

Nor do I seek any ups or downs, available to us all, that will "numb the pain". There is no "around". There is only "through". Use it. Make it a gift, a lesson. Empower yourself with it.

I open myself to the wisdom of the books. I focus on feeding my mind with positive imagery and on new perspectives for learning. Each of us has his or her own sources of inspiration and information to which we are individually drawn, and to these we must faithfully turn.

Know that you are *not* a victim, though it can feel like that and that belief can be easily justified. The inner dialogue of the victim is not unlike the seductive voice of the siren mermaids who called to the sailors causing them to forget their sense of direction and follow these alluring voices to their deaths on the rocks at sea. Casting ourselves as "the victim" can trap us into taking no responsibility. Thus the slippery slope of not having to Do the Work, feeding the notion that one's power (and lack of it) comes from outside, not from within.

I provide myself with music I love and flowers that delight and warm baths with lavender and eucalyptus oils mixed together, or by themselves. Geranium rose sprinkled under the flowing warm water beckons me to the healing richly scented tub. Soaking rehydrates, as well as relaxes. When I step out I visualize whatever was bothering me going down the drain. Gone!

I talk with friends and family, with whom my life is so richly blessed, who love and understand me and share their wisdom, experience, insights and encouragement. Some of us might seek counsel from a therapist or minister or a trusted family doctor.

I scrutinize my own thoughts, weeding out the ones that replay the drama, and focus instead on cultivating positive images and positive thoughts. I rely on the power of prayer, and turn to affirmations when I flag and need support. I try not to judge, while still honoring my feelings. I search to see how I contributed to the crisis, and what I need to learn. I ask what communication tools or insights I lacked in the situation that I might learn so next time I am better prepared. I seek quiet, not noise. I steep myself in the blessing of it.

I hug the animals, coo in their ears, run my hands over their gentle furry warm bodies and gratefully receive their kisses and affections.

Sometimes I find a change of scenes is good. I focus on fun, not to distract myself from my process, or to avoid the truth, but simply to nurture myself in a stimulating way. I like to hike around the lake, allowing the wind to surround me as I rhythmically walk, sweeping away any residual energies that clutter my being. Walking somehow integrates the shift toward normalcy, claiming my body, my feelings, and my power as my own.

I turn to writing. Delete. Write again. Delete again if necessary. Write again. I watch myself digging my way through the piles of leaves and debris and moving gently, lovingly toward my center, my clear mind, my clearer heart, my stable, loving authentic self, and leaving the rest behind.

I slip gently back into the rhythm of my own routine, the one I had before the storm swept through. I light candles. I clean house, always wrapping up that process with the burning of sage and then a sweet incense like frankincense or rose. Cleanliness and orderliness are important reflections of our inner state, and lack thereof equally reflects our inner condition.

It is when we most need our healing practices that we might find them most difficult to implement. Begin with one step. Judge yourself not. Take one more step and then another. Check in with yourself and see if you find yourself healing, however slowly. Be gentle. Be kind. Acknowledge yourself for each positive, self-loving act. Make certain you have a list, a guide, some skills and resources to turn to. And you work your way through. The *I Ching* counsels, "The best way to fight evil is to make energetic progress in the good."

What is it, dear ones, you turn to that nurtures you in the face of pain or sorrow or the sudden desolate storm?

MOVE GENTLY AMONG BEES

It took me a really long time to become comfortable with what I learned were scout bees that would find me walking in the woods and would accompany me for a short distance (which always felt too long) circling me in a wide girth around my head, about three feet out, circling, circling, checking me out. When I first had this experience my inclination was to swat at them, or duck or move more quickly, trying to avoid them. Once I understood that they simply wanted to explore and investigate me as I moved through their terrain, I began to be able to hold my center and keep my pace and allow them to complete their task without fearing I would be stung. Indeed, sticking with my own rhythm and my own intention, not allowing what they were doing to interfere with what I was doing, in actuality, probably ensured that I would not be stung.

I am a small child living with my grandparents in northern Ohio. I walk through winter's cold the few blocks to school by myself. On the way I must pass the city orphanage. One morning a Negro girl a little older than I steps out from the orphanage sidewalk and joins my stride. She is also going to school, though I don't remember her. I have never talked to a Negro girl before. I learn her name is Mary. I look up at her as we walk and I am fascinated by her skin and I can barely take my eyes off her full lips which I find very wonderful. My morning walks to school now include a note of anticipation that perhaps I will see Mary again and be able to walk with her, and many mornings do not disappoint, and I am happy for her interesting quiet company.

One evening I mention this to my grandparents at dinner. I am confused and embarrassed when I am met with a deafening silent wall of shock. My grandmother merely says, "It's better if you don't walk to school with Mary." I love my grandparents who care well and deeply for me. I have no idea what I have done to displease them, but I am mortified. I listen to them and I refrain from walking with Mary, though I feel sad, bewildered and ashamed.

Last Easter I decided to go to one of the oldest churches in our small town in North Carolina for services. I had never been there before. I arrived early, parked easily, and stepped inside and moved to the front so I could see. It was a splendid well-crafted church with stained glass windows on four sides set into walls of stone. I took a place in one of the old wooden pews next to a well-dressed Southern gentleman and his family, and sat quietly watching the others arrive. Suddenly a man approached the pew, looked at me and I heard him say, "What's going on here?" and he left as quickly as he had appeared. "Is there a problem?" I asked the gentleman seated next to me. "He's just used to sitting in this pew." "Oh," I said, feeling strangely uncomfortable. They have their own pews. I was not accustomed to attending a church where families had their own pews.

I looked around the church at the people assembling. I could not recall being in any environment ever that was so utterly Anglican. I felt I could easily have been in the United Kingdom, and I saw the irony of how at home genetically I was. These were, afterall, people of my own heritage. On the outside, at least, I fit. On the inside I felt a bit ill at ease.

I was relieved, actually, when I looked up and saw an attractive young black woman entering a door towards the front of the church. She stood next to the large wooden door and looked around. She reached down and put out her hands, and I suddenly realized she was pushing a wheelchair for a white woman and something in me was crestfallen. Men from the church found a place in front for the woman in the wheelchair, but the black woman was still looking for a place to sit. I scanned the pews toward the front of the church. There were empty places in the pews but no one offered the woman a seat. I felt my agitation and anxiety rise.

I leaned over toward the gentleman to my right, my elected guide in this environment.

"Am I looking at what I think I'm looking at?" I asked him.

"I think you are," he whispered.

The black woman continued to await a place to sit, maintaining her quiet dignity, but my blood by now began to boil. I could not, would not sit quietly and be a witness to this. A man finally brought the woman a folding chair which he placed at the end of the pew. The woman graciously sat down on the chair. My eyes kept moving from the black woman beautifully dressed sitting obligingly in the folded chair and the empty spaces in the pew adjacent to the chair and what I was seeing would not compute in my mind or heart.

I stood up abruptly and walked out of the church, tears flooding my eyes. I burst through the heavy wooden doors into the sunlight of morning, breathing in sharply the outside air. I found myself suddenly in small pod of people all wearing white robes, surrounded by men of duty wearing their Sunday suits. A woman in a white robe saw my face and questioned me.

"I'm really upset, " I told her. Why, she wanted to know. I wanted to leave. I did not want to interfere. I just wanted to go away. I apologized and started to move from the group, by now noticing me and wanting to know what had happened. I told them. A man in a suit angrily said to me, "You'd better know what is going on before you say things like this," and he stormed into the church to find out what had happened to the black woman. Like a swarm of agitated bees they surrounded me, all moving to action to investigate my claim.

"That seat in the pew is being saved for someone," they said and they invited me back into the church, rushing in and out, bees about my head and heart, working with their clan. A big to-do was made of finding me a seat at the back and a young man gestured to me to join their row. I moved in as he indicated and I realized at once he was giving up his seat for me. I protested but he insisted. Wanting to minimize what had become a fuss I sat down in this seat and he moved under an adjacent arch, standing, arms crossed.

I found myself sitting next to an elderly woman of much refinement, dressed principally in black and diamonds. She suddenly placed her beautiful wrinkled hand upon mine, leaned toward me and whispered in my ear, "It's too bad about Bill."

Bewildered, I asked, "Bill?"

"Yes," she said. "His father died early this morning."

I am sitting in the pew trying to digest the activities of this hive that have taken place over the previous quarter hour. I am slowly understanding several things. First, that the young man who has just chivalrously given me his seat has lost his father only hours before. I make what amends I can by insisting half an hour later that he take back his seat. He allows himself the dismantling of his Southern gallant upbringing enough to reclaim the seat he so desperately needed, more than I.

I am in a culture I do not understand. There are people playing by rules and agreements here that are foreign, as foreign as if I had left the country. If I am to survive I must quietly observe as much as possible, try not to speak. To listen as long and hard as I can, as deeply as I can. I must be a good anthropologist, or entomologist. Or something. I am not on my territory. This is not my hive. However much I look like these people on the outside, I am made of different stuff on the inside.

How do we move among the bees in our lives in a way that graciously acknowledges our differences while remaining true to our core?

INVEST IN TREES

My daughter was making her first journey to Appalachia! And knowing we would not see each other that Christmas I leapt at the chance to create a holiday with her in October. Fortunately Halloween is one of my favorite holidays of the year, upon which I could readily build, with vast support from the magnificent changing of leaves in a North Carolina fall.

I called a tree farm outside Asheville inquiring if he had "anything that looked like a Christmas tree". Puzzled, he asked why. "Do you really want to know?" I responded, grinning into the phone. He did. I explained that my daughter was coming, that it was her first trip to North Carolina, that I did not anticipate seeing her that Christmas, and that I wanted to make us a pumpkin tree. This man knew how to hear a mother's heart. Clearly touched, he invited me to come out, even though it was a wholesale business, and he would "find me something". I drove myself out into the country with my dog, and eventually spotted the long red gate he had given me as a landmark. I pulled through the gate and found myself entering a magical environment of all manner of trees in pots. I had never been to such a tree farm before, and I was instantly enchanted. When I exited from the car a warm young man came out to greet me, anticipating who I was. He indicated I should follow him and I followed his lead through pots and pots of trees, about which I could scarcely contain my curiosity, until we stopped before what appeared to be some kind of small and noble cedar. I felt strangely comfortable with its green upward spiraling flat branches. It was a narrow tree, about five and a half feet high, and he called it an *arborvitae*. "Tree of life," I smiled excitedly. "I'll take it!" When I arrived home I wetted it down, then brought it inside (promising the tree it was only for a few days) and began the joyful task of wrapping smiling round pumpkin lights about its limbs, then topping it off with a long strand of shiny red and gold tiny autumn leaves. I plugged in the pumpkin lights and stood back to admire my creation: A Pumpkin Tree! I grinned with glee and anticipation of my surprise. A couple of welcoming gifts wrapped in orange and gold papers with Halloween stickers strategically placed about the packages finished off the project. When Antonia arrived, tired from the long journey, the tree stood in a living room corner in shining festive welcome and as she spotted it, her weary face broke into a broad grin. I was so tickled, so pleased.

So now I own two trees. My ginkgo and a Western Red Cedar, as it turns out, which, curiously, really belongs in the Pacific Northwest. Nomadic as I am known to be, I am the owner and caregiver of two trees, who will now make their way with me in my travels. Somehow they give me great comfort. I fantasize, and have spoken with family members about placing these trees in our family cemetery plot. Here lie my greatgrandmother and greatgrandfather and grandmother and greataunt, and a bevy of cousins are buried nearby, throughout the small town cemetery. The plot was purchased over one hundred years ago for us by my greatgrandfather, a true investment in a longterm proposition, which is, in fact, what a tree is about. One day perhaps I will be buried there and my body, first purified in the grace of fire, will become part of these trees I nurture, who in return nurture me.

The trees in my life are not all physical and recognizable trees. There are the traditions, maintained devotedly year to year, creating the substance of family memories on which we hang our lives. Chai on Christmas morning. Gingerbread and popovers and the familiar ornaments that carry their special memories year after faithful year. Graves tended. Birthdays honored. Scrapbooks and photo books marking the passages of life. A wedding veil passed from grandmother to daughter to sister to grandchild. Stories long told from generation to generation, each word repeated faithfully as it was first heard by a grandchild or greatgrandchild. Such is the stuff of families, the roots of which go long and deep before us.

Who and what are the proverbial trees in your life to which you make the faithful annual pilgrimages? What does the honoring of these longheld traditions give in return? How does change or turning away from them affect your heart and soul? How can they be maintained, tended, and cared for in a world that will not stand by waiting for us, but catapults us further into a future we cannot predict, that we cannot count on to stay the same? What will you take in your hand, your heart, your being to sustain you on this ever-changing road, the trees of your life that lend substance, courage, strength, rootedness, and meaning?

HARVEST SEEDS FOR
FUTURE GARDENS

After two years in North Carolina, I had made the decision to return to the West. Strangely, I knew one of the things I would miss about North Carolina were the chipmunks. I didn't recall ever seeing any in California, and I was certain had they been about I would have noticed them. In Appalachia they were very abundant. The property on which I lived was a perfect haven for them as there was a small compact forest behind the house, and many trees lined the front as well. Their burrows were everywhere. I found the entrances to them as I gardened, round small gaping holes, often unprotected, sometimes beneath a plant or along a rock wall. Having researched them a bit I found this is rather uncommon so I had only to think that they felt quite unthreatened there by any predators and they made no great attempts to disguise the doorways to their underground homes. Finding them utterly enchanting and curious and elusive I had begun the practice of leaving them bits of nuts and sunflower seeds on one of two flat rocks in the back garden, just below the bedroom window so that I might secretly watch them. In the fall I knew their urgency to store what they needed to sustain themselves through what will undoubtedly be a particularly fierce winter was heightened. I was happy to contribute some small fare to their store, though I took comfort in the knowledge that their environment provided an abundance of acorns, seeds and berries to readily sustain them.

Chipmunks are quite lively and dart about like no other creature I ever observed. They are very well wired for survival, as they are extremely sensitive to the slightest movement, and disappear almost faster than the human eye can track. When I first moved to North Carolina and didn't know of their presence my early encounters with them were almost disconcerting. I would think, "What was that?" not quite sure what just streaked past. I have actually read they are known to be quite approachable in some territories, but this must be in areas where tourists are common to them and they have learned they will be fed by folks. On that property they were very untamed and unaccustomed to interacting with people and remained extremely wary, which was to their benefit. I confess I had hoped to establish some bit of trust over time with my contribution as they were so adorable, and I would like to have more chance to observe them. I remain grateful for the fleeting moments when I watched them discover what I left them this morning or that, as I peered ever so quietly from the bedroom window behind a curtain. With the tiniest movement on my part they were gone in a flash. But if I was able to remain very very still I had the luxury of watching them pick up a walnut and review it round and round with their teeth, making sure it has no pod or shell to remove, then pop it into their expanding cheeks, only to pick up another which joined the first and so on, until their swelled cheeks were expanded to the limit. Then they did one of two things, which I found quite interesting. Some they took down their tunnels to a nest they had created of grasses, bits of leaves and the soft down of certain kinds of flowers, such as the dandelion fluff we are so fond of blowing to the wind. And they buried this portion of nuts and seeds just underneath their grassy nest, where it would be available to them when the weather became very cold and snows covered those gaping entrances to their burrows and they lay in torpor till spring beckoned them back into the garden where they would resume their charming race about again. But another portion of their store they buried about the garden or forest floor, maybe to be reclaimed, should they find it in the hungry spring. But some will not be found, and some of these seeds will sprout in the sun's warmth the next year, and contribute to the landscape a tree or bush or plant that otherwise might not ever have emerged. We have the chipmunks to thank for this.

What seeds do we harvest and plant for future gardens? What is it we leave behind not to be reclaimed for ourselves but for those we leave behind? What part do we play in the scheme of the larger plan, acknowledging our connectedness not with that which we see about us, but with what comes even after we are gone?

RECYCLE EVERYTHING

Once in the space of one summer I was asked to sing at four different death ceremonies. One of them was in honor of my friend Dino's mother. He had decided he wanted to walk back into the woods above the small town in which we all lived and he would gently and lovingly release her ashes. As a group of us accompanied him up the hill in solemn silence I remember that I was suddenly overcome with emotion and tears rolled down my cheeks. My friend noticed and stepped back to console me. How could I tell him it was not for his mother's loss of life for which I was crying? It was for the unexpected realization that it was she who was going home.

I am at that age that my peers are just beginning to leave. Mostly it's parents of friends who are leaving, but there are those my own age whose lives are ending as well. Recently I received an emailed photo from a friend. Four well seasoned folks stood at ocean's edge. And at the end stood a young man with a small urn held in his hands, containing the ashes of his mother which they were about to cast off to the sea she loved in life so well. I had met his mother, a German woman, a friend of a friend. I had followed her slow demise and heard of her passing and of the subsequent ceremony her friends had created in her honor. They apparently met her body at the crematorium, filled the container to the brim with flowers and stood by lovingly in concert as the vessel of her being was transformed by the flames of fire. Here was the photo of the end of that chapter, coming to me from Baja California, her second home.

I have thought about these things. When one spends six years of one's life taking care of a parent in a nursing home, living a goodly portion of one's life among the elderly and dying, one of the gifts inherent in that process is to squarely ponder one's passing. There really is nowhere to hide. Thank you, Grandma.

One of the things that came out of that experience was to motivate me to prearrange what will be done with my body when I leave this Earth. I am in the throes of designing and purchasing my own headstone. It is a rather gritty task, but one in which I am becoming increasingly more interested and engaged. It's alternately sobering, humorous and creative. I spoke at some length with a man who designs and arranges such things. (Do you know you have to proofread headstones?) He showed me a wondrous black granite madonna who had just arrived from India. This process is far more interesting than one might have thought. We just mostly don't.

My friend Joanna, who has trained hospice workers, says that those of us who have tended to this task live our lives differently, more fully. I have joked with friends that while I may be a global nomad I own the piece of property I know I will be needing for sure: the family plot. Something in me takes comfort in knowing this. It puts my life in proper perspective.

One evening I was visiting with an acquaintance, a nurse, and I revealed to her that I would be cremated. I told her that part of my ashes would be buried in our family plot, next to my own ancestors, but that it was my deepest desire to have set aside a fund for my daughter to take my remaining ashes to all the places on this Earth that I have loved the most. To the sea in Acapulco. To the canals of Holland. To the shores of Puerto Rico. To the mountains and valleys of both Northern and Southern California. And thus to carve out a sacred time to review these treasured places, and to leave a bit of me behind in each and to express a deep gratitude on my behalf. What a splendid tribute to a global life!

The woman I spoke with quietly listened in warm appreciation. In that moment her husband who had been sitting near by tending to some task, stepped forth. Slowly he spoke. "I have been listening to what you have been saying. And I have to think. If I were to do the same thing you are suggesting, if I were to die today, I think I would have to tell them to pour my ashes over my computer. And that makes me very sad."

We sat in awkward silence embracing his pain in our hearts.

CELEBRATE THE FRUITS
OF YOUR LABORS

As it so happens, tonight is Halloween. While we often hear that Halloween was previously known as Hallow's Eve, this ancient holiday actually has its roots in an ancient Celtic harvest festival, called Sahmain [SO-wen], the last of three yearly Celtic festivals associated with bringing in the harvest. The First Harvest, Lugnasadh, corresponded with August's harvesting of barley, oats and wheat, and the Second Harvest, Mabon, focused on September's harvesting of apples, the primary fruit which would sustain the farmers and their families throughout the winter. By the time Samhain arrived at the end of October, food supplies were in and people were facing the harsh realities of winter. Samhain marked both the beginning of the Celtic year, while at the same time the last fading window of light and opportunity. Bonfires were built and people gathered together. From this bonfire each family took fire and returned to their homes and lit the hearth from this common source to ward off the darkness of winter. The veil between the worlds was regarded as very thin at this time, thus the current mystique around Halloween, dating back many many centuries.

In honor of these ancient traditions, this morning I cut a crisp green apple into small sections which I hung in various branches in the crab-apple tree outside my office window. I will peek from time to time today and see who has come to feast, expecting both the ever present squirrels and whatever birds are still about, and there are many. I included my precious little chipmunks in my ritual, leaving bits of apple and extra sunflower seeds on two flat stones that mark the entrance to a burrow just below my back deck. There is much to celebrate in my life this year and these small acts perhaps will not do them justice, but they are offered in love, thus well intentioned and my gratitude is not withholding.

In centuries past when agricultural people's lives and work and rhythms were tied to the land and to the dictates of the seasons, there were naturally advantageous and organic times to honor and give thanks for another year's work well done, usually in the late summer and fall. As each food source came to its fullness there was cause to celebrate as the people harvested their bounty. It was at this time they assessed their food supplies that ensured survival through the winter. There was good cause to be grateful. And they did this together, as a village, as a people, which is very difficult for us to imagine.

As we live our lives increasingly divorced from the natural energies of the Earth, and increasingly from each other, we no longer benefit from the deep and abiding community traditions of yore that found their impulses and boundaries contained within the seasons. We no longer all go to sleep when the sun goes down and all rise with the dawning of the sun. The moon powerful enough to create the tides of the sea is blithely defied by the body of a woman on birth control pills. The fascinating watering hole around which we currently gather is largely social media. As exciting and promising as this is, it is simultaneously not hard to understand how we might suffer some existential disconnect from the natural environment in which we actually physically live. Rather than our lives working in sync with nature, and reaping the benefits, our goal is often to transcend nature. It is against this backdrop that we seek to acknowledge and honor our work.

The gardener is blessed to maintain this connection. The gardener feels the earth in her hands, tends the emerging seed, nurtures her garden to abundance and harvests with joy the fruits of her labor as each plant she has planted comes to fruition. She knows the limits and confines and blessings of the season.

Winter is nearly upon me. I learned the benefits of pinestraw from my Southern neighbors and am putting certain plants to bed by gently placing handfuls of this blessed stuff about their roots. I am filled with gratitude for the warmth of summer, for the flowers that graced my life and I quietly celebrate the benchmarks I have met along the way.

CULTIVATE PLANTS WHICH ATTRACT LOVELY COMPANY

One of the best decisions I made this year was to plant several butterfly bushes along a strip of land that lies between the forest behind our house and the sidewalk. All manner of butterflies came to visit, many of which I had never seen before. Even more endearing to me are the bumblebees (my favorite bugs) who clamor over the periwinkle on the back bank, gathering nectar from the sweet simple blue flowers. This year I researched them and followed their comings and goings more closely, discovering to my great delight that they had a nest in the stone wall just outside my office. I had no idea they did this. I also discovered a woman in the United Kingdom who actually catches bumblebees and writes numbers on their furry backs and tracks them. A very scientific kind of thing. Who knew?

And who has not delighted in hummingbirds flocking en masse to a row of bottlebrush hedging or some irresistible bush or flower to their liking?

The garden is a wonderful place, indeed, to ponder the power we have in determining what shows up in our spaces simply through the very concerted and imaginative selections we are free to make.

And how does this translate into other realms?

Say, dogs?

The first time I saw a Border Collie I was rummaging around in the woods behind my house in Little River, where I had just moved, just across from the raging Pacific sea which hammered against the rough cliffs of Mendocino County. I was poking around the base of a tree where I spotted a small pinkish wild orchid, when suddenly out of seemingly nowhere, as I stood up I saw a very strong, very fast dog charging toward me, barking furiously. I was very frightened, but all I could think to do, strangely enough, was to squat down and welcome him. This is not anything I would recommend, normally, but this is what I did. The dog continued to charge through the forest but he was slightly disarmed at my lowered posture, one I guess I was hoping would convey I was not a threat, and hopefully not looking any more like prey. And it worked. The dog slowed his pace as he gained upon me, and thankfully his owner, a small imp of a woman, appeared and called him. He backed off.

Thus began a very rich chapter of my life which continues to this day titled Border Collies. That day in the woods led me to the discovery of Moxie and later to Peaches, and then to Conner and Ruby.

One of the most fun things in the world was going to the beach with the Border Collies, The four of us would happily hit the beach together. We would clamber down the sides of sandy, rocky cliffs of three counties, and the dogs would tear down to the waves, looking for bits of driftwood or even seaweed for us to throw along the sea's edge which they would chase after with passion and gusto and bring back for us to throw again. They ran up and down the upper beach, taking in everything with their noses at once, breathing in the sea's fresh salt air, expressing the beauty and grace and freedom of movement, racing in the wind, always mindful of their owners' whereabouts, though they sometimes rushed several hundred yards in front of us, exuberant in their freedom to run and to play.

And then there are the Dog Trials. For anyone who has not been to a Border Collie Trial, I recommend it. To witness these most amazingly intelligent of dogs working in their natural environment, herding sheep into pens with the most subtle direction from their masters is to open one's perceptions of dogs into an entirely new realm.

Border Collies were bred for their intelligence. There is not to date too much pressure regarding conformity on their looks and thank goodness. They remain somewhat outside the rigid confines of these kinds of considerations, though they are edging in this direction, much to the chagrin of many breeders and owners of these wonderful dogs.

Witnessing what takes place at a trial is a very old practice with its roots largely in the British Isles. Culturally there is a vast difference from continent to continent how these trials are conducted. In Britain rather refined looking gentlemen are about on the turf, wearing jackets and tweed hats and whistling crisply their commands at a distance. The American version, at least in the West, is much as you might expect, the cowboy version with lots of trucks and hats and bandanas. But at the eye of these trials is the focused intention of a dog who has faithfully tended sheep for man for over two centuries. And at the heart of that focus is the Border Collie stare. They know when to move in, when to back off, when to lie low, when to stand, where to move the sheep, how fast, how slow. They know left from right, green from red. Their vocabularies are very large and they are very responsive. And the breeders and trainers are a hardy lot, grounded, independent and dedicated to the preservation of this very distinct and worthy breed.

Border Collies are not for the timid or weak-willed. They need an alpha handler. They will outsmart you if you can't stay on top of them. They are energetic and need lots of exercise. But, oh, the friends you meet, and the trails you walk, and the unlikely doors that open.

What beloved creatures of this precious planet Earth do you invite into your life that as a result bring you joy and adventure and open doors to places and beings you would not otherwise encounter?

FEED AND WATER AT OPTIMUM TIMES

Recently a business acquaintance emailed me that she had just planted her first garden! She knew I would be pleased to hear. She is from The City and she apparently had never had a garden before and she was very excited. She said she planted it with her boyfriend in a six foot wooden box. And she planted only herbs. Then she revealed the most endearing part of her story: that she had been watering her plants in the heat of the afternoon because she "thought they were hot". I could see a city girl identifying with a plant thinking the heat of the afternoon sun required a good shower!

On the practical level gardeners learn early on that plants generally need to receive water either early in the morning when evaporation is minimal, or perhaps evenings, being careful, however, not to allow, say, roses, to go to bed with wet leaves. They hate it.

The truth is we are just as complex as the flowers. Some of us are roses. Some of us are daisies. Some of us are sunflowers. The important thing isn't necessarily to find some outside advice about the best thing to do. The important thing is to know yourself well enough to know what is the best thing to do for *you*. Some of us are night people, some of us early risers. There are no hard and fast rules that are going to work for all of us, though it would probably be safe to say it's not wise to go to bed having just devoured a large late dinner. And some of us cannot abide heavy breakfasts. Many of us create house rules and we simply don't eat past a certain time. I used to have a rule that I never ate past 6:00 PM. I was thin as a beanpole. But I was a nymph who danced four nights out of seven! Now I generally follow similar habits (having traded in the heavy dancing for swimming and yoga) but I'm more flexible.

What is important is that we bring our full awareness to our habits, without judging (the hardest part!) and move ourselves in the right direction, gradually over time. I believe that the sheer power of being consciously aware of our actions (even the teeniest ones) is a big step in the right direction. Noticing is powerful. Even noticing without changing is powerful. Noticing *is* change. By noticing, and "just" noticing, we will begin to improve. An example of how this shows up in my life is realizing, "Oh, that's interesting. I don't eat cookies anymore." And I don't. Or, oh that's interesting, I don't eat bread much anymore. And I don't. I move towards eating higher quality foods which I realize are high octane fuels for my body. It's not always linear and consistent, but overall the movement is towards improvement. I know it's in vogue to call in the Food Police and Get With the Program. And maybe sometimes that is appropriate in some desperate situations. But feeding and watering at appropriate times could begin simply with writing it all down. Bring your awareness to your situation. And design what works for you, special you. And be patient with yourself. This path I believe leads to long-term effective change that is in keeping with an integrated ever deepening self respect and self love. I believe it works because it is an authentic process, that is true to the self.

Not only do we have our physical bodies to feed and water, we also have our emotional, mental and spiritual planes to feed (and, isn't it easy to mix them up?!). It is astounding and overwhelming to think of the million gazillion stories that make up our individual lives and how we have been deliberately or randomly "fed" mentally, emotionally and spiritually, sometimes richly, sometimes poorly, depending, as adults, by our conscious (or unconscious) choices. Ultimately we have free will and we must each determine for ourselves what it is and how it is we feed ourselves on all the various levels that we are required to feed ourselves (or not) in this lifetime.

Is the amount of time spent on feeding the physical body in balanced proportion to the amount of time we feed our emotional, mental and spiritual bodies? We might be well served by taking a gentle look at the actual amounts of time we spend in each category and see if something in our lives is out of balance. And it is here in this area we are most apt to become confused. We are rushed, under pressure, and some part of us recognizes that we are hungry. We reach for food to fill that hungry need. Had we taken the time to reflect a bit, either through journaling or quiet meditation we might have discovered that the hunger we were experiencing really didn't require that hamburger or cookie. The hunger we were vaguely aware of in our haste was asking for being touched and the food it needed to fill it was actually reaching out to our partners or a friend, asking for a hug, or scheduling a massage! Maybe our restlessness which we stuffed with an extra helping at dinnertime was actually a hungry muffled voice longing for a vacation or maybe just a walk around the park? Maybe the hunger lives in your lungs and you are longing for fresh air. Or maybe it resides in your heart and soul and you need to make music. In short, there are many kinds of hungers and it takes a quiet mind to get the right food to the right internal voice at the right time.

Cultivating this awareness might begin by asking a couple of seemingly simple questions, like "Who within me is hungry and what is it she needs?" Or, "Who within me is reaching for this candybar and what is it he really needs?" And maybe it is the candybar. And maybe not, and you still reach for the candybar (without judgment!) but you took the first step towards awareness and this could be for you an important shift. Maybe next time you notice you grab a protein bar instead. Maybe not. But you bring your awareness along for the ride. You don't do it unconsciously anymore.

Feeding the mind, heart and soul, all at the appropriate times is an art. It is the stuff our lives are made of, the texture, the cut, the design. How is it that you feed and water yourselves, your whole selves, and what is the perfect timing for you as an individual? On the most basic of levels, are you wolfing down low quality foods (or even high quality foods), literally or metaphorically, and expecting these substances to sustain you, to bring out the best in you? Or have you found an even, sound rhythm to your nurturance, inner and outer, that creates a life well lived, with no regrets?

KNOW AND INCLUDE A WIDE
VARIETY OF SPECIES IN YOUR GARDEN

I don't know where the expression Pig Heaven comes from, but whenever I have lived in the country, that's where I've been. In Pig Heaven. One of the greatest joys of having lived at the end of a dirt road on four acres of property in the woods was that I really could have as many animals as I wanted — and was surrounded by other people's animals, as well as the ones who lived there in their natural habitat. We lived among them, I often reminded myself. They arrived first, and I tried to abide respectfully with that in the front of my mind.

My own extended creature tribe grew to include that gorgeous Bantam rooster, Chanticleer, whom you will recall I found camped out bravely in the woods, wisely next to a stream, and his girlfriend, Henny Penny; two English budgies; the 23 canaries; the cats: spunky old Amelia and my precious Honeypot, and later, Luna, the Maine Coon showcat and my beloved Border Collies, Moxie and Peaches.

Adding to my joy were my neighbors' animals with whom I shared various fences. I fondly visited Cheyenne the donkey, whose pasture butted up against my apple orchard near the entrance to my property. Handy for her. And how I treasured the 32-year-old sway back horse belonging to my German neighbors who lived just below, all without the direct and daily responsibilities of taking care of either of them. I was like the auntie, who called friendly greetings and offered the occasional apple, allowing them to munch their way to their own Pig Heaven.

One of my very favorite adventures with Cheyenne was the day I decided to include her in a photo shoot I did for a visiting Mexican mariachi band in exchange for their playing their lively music at my daughter's 30th birthday party. The band returned a week later in full costume, complete with black embroidered jackets and wide matching sombreros and I marched them all down to the orchard in the hot sun and lined them up along the fence, with Cheyenne occupying the center of the photos. I take great delight knowing she is likely now gracing the cover of this mariachi band's latest CD somewhere in Guadalajara, unbeknownst to her owners.

Not limited to domestic animals, my kingdom included a restless fox who arrived on Christmas Eve only to pace up and down the dirt drive that ran before my front door for a full ten minutes. I don't know why.

Deer traipsed through almost daily, including a spectacular young buck with large proud points who allowed me to photograph him one bright spring afternoon as he stood alertly facing me in the garden in front of my guest cabin. Wild turkeys came often and voraciously cleaned up the corn spill from Chanti and Henny Penny's pens. They would surround the pens in a scarf of feathers and give new meaning to the word gobble, and having eaten the last crumb, would depart, only to return to scavenge another day. Coyotes threaded their way through the warp and woof of daily life in the woods. Each bore different energies, and different agendas, a good lesson. Some could be trusted. Others certainly could not and I would protectively draw the cats closer to the hearth.

As each animal crossed my path I researched. I hit the Net. I looked them up. I read about each one, expanding my knowledge of their habits, their lives, their inclinations. I dispelled wives' tales I'd heard as a child. I educated neighbors who eyed their guns when the coyotes and wild turkeys passed through. I learned to better trust my own instincts. This coyote is here for apples. That one is here for cats or anything else it can churn into energy to survive.

Sitting on the bank one afternoon just out of reach beyond the flimsy wire fence sat, what? A cat? No. A grey fox. Staring at me. I retired to the house, somewhat shaken. Still, the frame of the sighting was precious. Strangers' cats crossed the land. Neighbors' cows drifted in. And out.

A mouse in the toilet at 2:00 AM. Really. I had almost sat down but noticed an unfamiliar shadow in the bowl, illuminated by the nightlight and turned on the overhead light just in time. What to do? Call the dogs. Sleepily the dogs peek into the toilet bowl. What do you want us to do? Do *something*! They try to rouse from their slumber, eyes barely open. It's a mouse. Yes, I know it's a mouse. In my toilet. Help me out. They try to respond but it's beyond their comprehension at this hour. A simple mouse. In the toilet. They go back to bed. In sleepy desperation, I flush the toilet. Twice. It's gone. Sometimes the most expedient and obvious solution is not what you really would want to have chosen under other conditions.

These adventures are now a firm part of my world, richly included among the many joys of my life. I deeply treasure having lived in the woods on the edge of the unknown, sharing my life, my chapters within the natural habitat of other creatures, my heart expanding with each interaction, as each lovely one entered the stage of my life, sharing with me, gracing me with their exquisite presence.

Each and every adventure I have chosen, dear readers, held within it the power to expand, to teach. The more I risked, the wider and more diversely I chose, the richer my experience and the more precious the gift. I have been so blessed. Aren't we all?

FINIS